Issues of the Ends of Life

The Segelberg Series

Terry Waite

Jocelyn Downie

Karen Lebacqz

Harvey M. Chochinov & Genevieve Thompson

Allan E. Blakeney

Eric Beresford

with a Preface by
Innis Christie

Introduction & Dedication by
David Stuewe

David Buley, editor

Trafford Publishing
Bloomington

Order this book online at www.trafford.com
or email orders@trafford.com

Most Trafford titles are also available at major online book retailers.

Printed in the United States of America.

ISBN: 978-1-4269-1250-4 (sc)
ISBN: 978-1-4269-1251-1 (hc)
ISBN: 978-1-4269-1252-8 (e)

This publication edited by David Buley, PhD

   1. Faith. 2. Death. 3. Public Policy. 4. Palliative Care.
   I. Buley, David. II. Series.

Trafford rev. 08/29/2013

 www.trafford.com

North America & international
toll-free: 1 888 232 4444 (USA & Canada)
fax: 812 355 4082

Contents

The Segelberg Series

on

Public Policy and Spirituality

Issues of the Ends of Life

The Reverend Dr. Eric Segelberg (1920–2001)

Introduction

David Stuewe

Chair of the Board of Directors of The Segelberg Trust

The Segelberg Series explores the intersection of religious faith and public policy. This book contains the lectures focused on The Ends of Life. Dalhousie University's School of Public Administration managed the series through a lecture committee under the able leadership of the former Dean of Dalhousie's Law School, Professor Innis Christie, QC.

The series was funded by a grant from The Segelberg Trust, which was established in 1984 by The Reverend Doctor Eric Segelberg (Dec 20, 1920, to Oct 17, 2001). Dr. Segelberg studied Theology and Classics at Uppsala and Oxford Universities. In 1968 he became a professor of Classics at Dalhousie University (Halifax, Nova Scotia, Canada) and taught there until his retirement in 1990. During his time teaching at Dalhousie, and his annual post-retirement autumn visits and seminars, he established an eclectic series of friendships in Halifax and the Maritimes.

Through those relationships, this thoughtful Swede was engaged in a continuing series of conversations exploring matters of principle and their translation into everyday life. Father Eric had an insightful mind, always a dry humour, and very generous spirit. He particularly enjoyed conversations focusing on theology, public policy and the environment. His objective in establishing The Segelberg Trust was to promote the understanding of Christianity and its relationship to his three keen interests— theology, public policy and the environment.

The Segelberg Trust's Board of Directors views the lecture series as a means to continue Father Eric's contribution to advancing understanding of issues of importance to society and particularly as they relate to the interplay of public policy and religious faith. The Trust will support lectures and public discussions dealing with the intercession of religious faith and public policy. Details on future Trust-supported lectures and discussions will be available on the Dalhousie University and The Segelberg Trust webpages dedicated to the Segelberg Series.

In his era, Father Eric was the youngest priest to be ordained in the Church of Sweden's history. He was first and foremost a humble priest who was an outstanding theologian, academic and friend to a wide circle throughout the world. The Segelberg Trust attempts to carry on Eric's commitment to service and exploration of ideas in public policy through this series, in the environment through support of Big Cove YMCA Camp and to theology through grants to the Atlantic Theological Conference.

The Segelberg Trust's Board (Jan Buley, Peter Harris, Gerry Schaus, David Stuewe and Robert Warren) is thankful for the assistance and participation of those who made this first Lecture Series a success. Gratitude is particularly extended to the School of Public Administration; The Segelberg Lecture Committee (Jan Buley, Marguerite Cassin, Innis Christie, Eric Beresford, David Stuewe and Oscar Wong) and the Segelberg Research Assistants (Tamara Krawchenko, Evan MacDonald, Craig O'Blenis and Melissa de Witt) who from 2005 to 2008 worked on this project. It was the desire of Father Eric that the community explore issues of importance in a respectful and informed manner. He would have enjoyed the meaningful conversations this series supported.

Dedication

Innes Christie (1937–2009)

I wasn't afraid of death.
Death is something that we shall all experience.
There will be no exceptions, of course. We shall all experience it and,
therefore, it seems to me to be totally pointless
to be afraid of death.
What I was afraid of was the way in which I would die,
the means by which I would die.

Terry Waite

Innis Christie did experience death far too early after a life focused on family, fun and service to humankind. He was a tireless worker standing tall for what he found to be the right thing to do, sharing knowledge and exploring the means to address difficult workplace situations. He undertook the latter both as a senior policy advisor to government and as a labour arbitrator.

At Dalhousie's Law School he helped a generation of lawyers understand the significant power disadvantage that confronted workers, and the importance of labour law in keeping societal order and fairness. His commitment to the development and practice of law in Canada was recognized at the national and provincial levels with the Bora Laskin Award and the Nova Scotia Barristers' Society's Distinguished Service Award.

The Segelberg Trust was fortunate that Innis was willing to turn his mind to other important societal questions. As chair of the Ends of Life Lecture Committee he, and the other committee members, brought together information and points of view, in a thoughtful and sensitive manner, to allow people to explore the means by which they might die. At the end of life people have little power over what is about to happen. Innis felt strongly that despite this power imbalance humans should have a say in how that end comes about.

This topic touches on legal, medical and spiritual issues. Understanding and considering the interplay of these matters is complicated. The Rev. Dr. Eric Segelberg would appreciate the opportunity to engage in these discussions. We hope that you will find this collection, which Innis so gracefully guided through his chairing of the committee that presented the series, to be helpful in your exploration and discussions of this very important issue.

Dedication

Innis Christie, born and brought up a Nova Scotian, studied at Dalhousie, Cambridge and Yale Universities. He had a broad view of the world and his introduction to this book was written while he was undergoing treatment for cancer. That cancer took him from us far too early in his life.

The Segelberg Trust wishes to thank Innis, and his family, for his commitment to the advancement of knowledge through open and respectful dialogue on sensitive issues. Such dialogue is important for the advancement of society. It is particularly important when addressing "the very simple human point," as Terry Waite called our fear of *"the way in which I would die, [and] the means by which I would die."*

David Stuewe
Chair, The Segelberg Trust

Preface

Innis Christie, QC
Chair, Segelberg Lecture Series

This first publication of the Segelberg Lecture Series explores the intersection of public policy and spirituality as it relates to the ending of human life. The lectures in this book range from Dr. Terry Waite's powerful narrative of facing death and maintaining life in seemingly endless captivity, through probing and profound discussions of termination of treatment, assisted suicide and euthanasia by Dr. Jocelyn Downie, Dr. Karen Lebacqz, Canon Eric Beresford and Hon. Allan Blakeney to the scholarly description of the latest research on dying with dignity in palliative care by Drs. Harvey Chochinov and Genevieve Thompson.

The lectures as published in this volume follow the sequence of their presentation at Dalhousie University to some 1700 participants. They start with, as Terry Waite said in his own words, "laying the table." He addresses the issues to be faced at the end of life as he saw them while held hostage by Hezbollah in Beirut for almost five years. Much of that time he was chained 24 hours a day in unlighted solitary confinement. Working for the Archbishop of Canterbury to free hostages, he was himself taken hostage. The full tale is told in his 1993 book *Taken on Trust*, published by Harcourt Brace.

Terry Waite tells us in his lecture that he was not afraid of death because it is "pointless to be afraid of death" since "we shall all experience it." His "simple human feeling" was fear of the means by which he would die. Spirituality was important to him, but he refused to pray, "Oh God, get me out of this situation." Rather, he fell back on his religious upbringing for "good language ... which breathes a certain harmony into the soul." He did not give up; he hung onto life for himself but even more for the sake of those for whom he cared. The values of love, compassion, care and understanding, which, he says, "lie at the heart, surely, of any religious tradition worth its soul," sustained him. In response to questions, he contrasted this with the other "stream" in religion, "the stream of power and command, compulsion," which he associated particularly with the rise of the religious right in the United States.

In the second lecture, "The Ends of Life and Death: Public Policy, Spirituality and the Law", Jocelyn Downie, Professor of Law at Dalhousie, addressed "euthanasia and assisted suicide." "Few words," she says, "take us more directly to the intersection of law and spirituality." Polarized positions "about the significance and legitimacy of autonomy and agency in relation to the timing and cause of death," she says, "are frequently justified through reference to various conceptions of human spirituality."

With care and lucidity Dr. Downie then describes the current legal status of the withholding and withdrawal of potentially life-sustaining treatment the provision of potentially life-shortening symptom relief, assisted suicide and euthanasia, and examines some of the arguments for the decriminalization of assisted suicide and euthanasia. These are elaborated more fully in her award-winning book *Dying Justice: A Case for Decriminalizing Euthanasia and Assisted Suicide in Canada* (University of Toronto Press, 2004). She concludes that assisted suicide and euthanasia, which are criminal, should have the same legal status as the withholding and withdrawal of potentially life-sustaining treatment, which are not. While Dr. Downie believes "that end-of-life law and policy is inextricably linked up with spirituality" she does not accept "that this leaves us victim to intractable conflict". She believes, it would seem rather optimistically, that "respectful engagement will lead most (although certainly not all) Canadians to conclude that the law should be changed."

Dr. Downie's "legal" lecture and the third and fourth lectures were followed by brief remarks from three commentators from the other perspectives brought to bear in this series. Senator Sharon Carstairs, former Leader of the Opposition in the Manitoba Legislature and former Minister with Special Responsibility for Palliative Care in the Federal Government of Canada, commented from the perspective of public policy, noting the sharp divisions in Canadian society. Dr. Marilyn Walker, Associate Professor of Anthropology at Mount Allison University, commented briefly on the diversity of cultural perspectives on the issues raised by Dr. Downie. Dr. Paul MacIntyre, Division Head of Palliative Medicine for the QEII Health Sciences Centre in Halifax, brought a medical perspective to the discussion. He stressed that for the vast majority of people facing the end of life the important issues addressed by Dr. Downie do not arise. For them appropriate palliative care, to which the series returned in the fourth lecture, is the issue.

In the third lecture Dr. Karen Lebacqz, Professor of Theological Ethics, Emerita, at the Pacific School of Religion, Berkeley, recounted in detail the controversy surrounding the well known case of Terri Schiavo, whose husband, for 15 years ending in 2005, fought her parents though the American courts over whether he could withdraw the feeding tube that was keeping her alive in a vegetative state, against her wishes according to him. The dispute became highly political, involving not only Governor Bush of Florida but also his brother, the President. The convoluted details of this public dispute, rooted in differing religious beliefs as well as personal hatred, political posturing and possibly different conceptions of love, may suggest that Jocelyn Downie's call in the second lecture for "respectful" engagement between those of different spiritual views, leading to a broad consensus, may be very optimistic, unless Canadian and American views on these issues are very different. Indeed, Dr. Lebacqz herself concludes that "autonomy is too narrow a base for law in the medical arena" because it underweights "relational truth." She quotes Terri Schiavo's brother as "tak[ing] relational truth seriously" when he said in *A Life That Matters*, a book written by her family in 2006, "We have obligations to each other and to God."

The first commentator on Dr. Lebacqz's lecture was Dr. Graeme Rocker of Dalhousie's Faculty of Medicine, a past president of the Canadian Critical Care Society, who chaired a policy subcommittee of that Society which produced a consensus document on the withholding and withdrawing of therapy. He called the Terri Schiavo case "the most appalling media driven spectacle I've witnessed in 28 years as a physician ... an incredible violation of her rights to privacy and the duty of confidentiality" owed by all involved. He agreed, however, with Dr. Lebacqz insofar as he said, "I accept and applaud a request that we do not treat individuals as if they were individuals operating in total isolation from the rest of the world [but] ... we have to be careful about which relationship matters most and to whom."

The second commentator on Dr. Lebacqz's lecture was Prof. David Blaikie of the Dalhousie Faculty of Law, who holds a graduate degree in religious studies and writes on religion and the law. He described the Terri Schiavo case as "at times bitter and repellent," and quoted a commentator who described it as involving "the politics of righteousness" in which one side has unshakeable convictions that they are right and that those on the other side are wrong; that they are morally good and the other side not. Like Dr. Downie in the second lecture, Professor Blaikie called for debate and discussion of public policy, with "real tolerance of differences engaged, explored and debated within the bond of a profound respect for the humanity of the other." "Judicial decisions," Blaikie concluded, "should not take the place of reasoned and respectful public debate and discussion."

The third commentator on Dr. Lebacqz's lecture was Dr. Gail Dinter-Gottlieb, who was then President of Acadia University. Having been asked to comment from the perspective of public policy, she briefly reviewed the high-level political and legal activity precipitated by the Schiavo case, which made the case of a dying woman a public issue In Dr. Dinter-Gottlieb's view, the issue was the division of church and state, which she said had been blurred in the preceding six years by the Bush presidency playing to the religious right. She stated that, even without a formal credo of separation of church and state, as in the American Constitution, no such political intervention would occur in Canada.

The fourth lecture, by Dr. Harvey Chochinov on palliative care, brought a quite different, less controversial perspective to the end of life. It is therefore appropriate to leave it aside for the moment and next introduce the dual fifth lecture, or two lectures, given by Hon. Allan E. Blakeney, former Premier of Saskatchewan and the Reverend Canon Eric Beresford, President of the Atlantic School of Theology, which address more directly the issues raised in the second and third lectures by Dr. Downie and Dr. Lebacqz.

Having been asked, as he said, to speak about the public policy issues that surround death and dying "which is in some way aided or abetted by some person other than the dear departed," Mr. Blakeney talked not so much about the substance of such issues as about the approach politicians take to such issues. "What," he asks, "should be the function of laws we make in this area?" and "How do we achieve the consensus or compromise which allows laws on death and dying to be widely acceptable?"

Mr. Blakeney's view, based on the history of similarly contentious laws at the nexus of public policy and religious faith with respect to adultery, birth control and same-sex marriage, is that the public continues to want the law both to set out workable rules "and to embody moral principles and values." "And that," he says, "is often tough to accomplish." On compromise, Mr. Blakeney rejects the "binary view of government" based on the percentage of the public that favours "yes" or "no," and creates streams of winners and losers. Citizens, he says, should be made to feel that citizenship is "an exercise in learning to get along with our fellow citizens in a pluralistic society."

On death and dying, Mr. Blakeney says, there are many differing views, shaped by differing beliefs, some sharply differing, about the nature of human life and the role, if any, of a deity—a fact those shaping public policy are well aware of. Rather than to try to argue for or against one side or the other, because the public's beliefs "are not fundamentally based on logic," the strong tendency of politicians will be to do nothing until public opinion has jelled. Paraphrasing Oliver Wendell Holmes Jr., "the life of public policy is not in logic but in experience." But, Mr. Blakeney concluded, we should try to change such laws to force public discussion, although policy makers will continue to seek answers that are acceptable "not because of the cogency of the reasoning but because they respond to deeply held and, regrettably, very different beliefs among citizens of our very diverse society."

In his scholarly and richly nuanced lecture, "The Ends of Life: Public Policy, Reason and Faith: A Theological

Contribution", Canon Beresford finds common ground with Mr. Blakeney when he says:

> The attempt to shape public policy in controversial areas is a thankless one at the best of times, but in areas where religious passions become engaged—areas like euthanasia and assisted suicide—public policy formation pretty quickly becomes bogged down....

He then asks, however, "is this really the result of the attempt to import narrowly religious concerns into public debate that need to be based on more generally shared, more rational grounds, or does the problem run deeper?" And deeper he goes. "In understanding the 'ends of life', the challenge," Canon Beresford says, "is not religion, it is ethics." But in our pluralistic society the ethical principles derived from the rationality espoused by "the culturally and historically particular values of the European Enlightenment ... were, at best, incomplete." In this context, he asks, what value can be found in the intervention of churches? In three broad areas he says they might be helpful. One religious contribution would be to clarify our underlying and shared values, and to expose the "inconsistencies and deceptions" in the accounts of those values.

Secondly, discussion of the legalization of euthanasia

> ...needs to be based on understandings of human will and human motives that are richer and more insightful than those often appealed to on either side of the debate. Religious categories—while not shared by all—may be helpful if they enable us to provide particularly rich and nuanced accounts of widely held consensus.

Thirdly, religious thinkers and religious communities might offer "significant insight into practices that make possible and sustain moral community." Here Canon Beresford joins with Dr. Downie, Dr. Lebacqz and Professor Blaikie in calling for more dialogue than debate in that "Dialogue begins in a recognition and affirmation of relationship and what it is we share together." "Consensus," he says, "is not something we notice as easily as disagreement because we are not provoked to discuss it."

Far less contentious and, as Dr. Paul MacIntyre pointed out in commenting on Dr. Downie's second lecture, much more frequently part of every life experience with death and dying, is palliative care. In the fourth Segelberg lecture, Dr. Harvey Chochinov, psychiatrist and Director of the Manitoba Palliative Care Research Unit of CancerCare Manitoba, spoke on "Dying With Dignity: A Contemporary Challenge in End of Life Care." The paper by Dr. Chochinov and Dr. Genevieve Thompson upon which Dr. Chochinov's richly illustrated and humane lecture was based addresses what is meant by dignity in dying and how health care providers might not only preserve but also augment dignity at this critical point. It presents a model of dignity in the terminally ill and its clinical implications.

Theoretical discussions have led to conclusions that seem correct intuitively, such as the notions that a sense of dignity is intimately tied to a person's ability to make rational choices and a sense of being a burden to others is highly correlated with loss of dignity. However, Dr. Chochinov tells us there has been a paucity of research exploring the concept of dignity at the end of life.

To help fill this gap, Dr. Chochinov and his colleagues systematically explored and built on a model of dignity in the terminally ill in which "an individual's perception of dignity is related to and influenced by three major areas: 1) illness-related concerns; 2) dignity-conserving repertoire; and 3) social dignity inventory, which is environmental factors, i.e. external factors which strengthen or undermine the patient's relationships with others. Perhaps most pertinent to this series of lectures is one of the aspects of #2—the "dignity conserving practice," which is described as "seeking spiritual comfort" by drawing on previously held religious or spiritual beliefs.

However, the two items most frequently endorsed by patients as relating to their sense of dignity were "not feeling treated with respect or understanding" and "feeling a burden to others." The dignity therapy developed and tested by Dr. Chochinov and his group focuses on providing patients with the opportunity to discuss aspects of their lives they feel most proud of, things they feel are or were most meaningful and the personal history they want remembered and allowing them to provide instruction on looking after their loved ones. These sessions are tape-recorded, transcribed, edited and returned to the patient. "The evidence is that the patients report a heightened sense of dignity, an increased sense of purpose, a heightened sense of meaning and an increased will to live."

Even without invoking full-blown dignity therapy, this model provides clinicians with guidance on how to approach dignity concerns. Using a simple A B C D mnemonic suggested by Dr. Chochinov, they should find out what matters to the individual patient, be it religious or spiritual beliefs, vocation or hobbies, and incorporate those concerns into their Attitude and Behaviour at the bedside, coupled with Compassion in a Dialogue in which the personhood of the individual, beyond his or her illness, is acknowledged.

The first commentator on Dr. Chochinov's lecture was the Reverend Cathy Simpson, who is engaged in PhD research in this area. Drawing on considerable experience comforting the dying, she said that "spirituality very much aligns with the kind of dignity-conserving approach Dr. Chochinov talked about." And spirituality in the Reverend Simpson's understanding is very much tied to relationships, the importance of which virtually all of the speakers in this series stressed. She is saddened by what she sees as the negative reputation with which traditional religious practices have been tarred because "for many, many people [they] bring meaning and comfort" and there is frequently a spiritual dimension to suffering at the end of life. Rev'd Simpson sees evidence of that within the empirical world of biomedicine, but quite apart from "best practices," she emphasized that spirituality is personal. Reflecting on Dr. Chochinov's argument for dignity-conserving care, Rev'd Simpson paraphrased William Butler Yeats: "But I being vulnerable have only my dignity. I have spread my dignity at your feet. Tread softly because you tread on my dignity."

The second commentator was Dr. Fiona Bergin, a lawyer, medical doctor and a past Director of Dalhousie's Health Law Institute. She spoke specifically about advanced directives, making the point that an advanced directive can be used to promote a dignified death. Advanced directives are a starting point, she said, for Dr. Chochinov's "D" (dialogue), and they tie in directly to the factors, like control and autonomy, that his research indicated enhance dignity in the dying. The advanced directive "becomes a vehicle by which goals of care can be adopted for the patient … to promote patient dignity and to ensure that their wishes are respected when they can no longer make their wishes known."

The third commentator on Dr. Chochinov's lecture was Brian Flemming, lawyer, journalist and public policy guru. Mr. Flemming cast something of a pall over Dr. Chochinov's picture of dying with dignity. He pointed out that the level of respect or dignity and control by the state, which funds the institutions in which most people now die, varies greatly from place to place and institution to institution. As he pointed out, the owners of for-profit institutions like nursing care places, or even the boards of not-for-profit ones, cannot be forced to provide more than minimum staffing, and minimums often become maximums. "Public policy," Mr. Flemming said, "can do little to engender or force an existential or spiritual dimension to death and dying." It is difficult enough for front-line workers to have the time to get to know the patients or residents they are caring for, let alone get to know them well enough "to discover where the wellsprings of their worth are and what they really value." In the medical world, demands for service are simply far out-stripping supply. If we cannot provide basic medical services, he asked, what hope is there for any well funded dying with dignity movement? He concluded that many who live dignified lives will die in dignity, but few who do not live in dignity will die in dignity.

I trust that this preview, even with this pessimistic closing note, will encourage you to read the Segelberg Lectures published here. If there is a single theme that dominates throughout, from all these differing perspectives on the nexus of public policy and spirituality in relation to death and dying, it is the importance of open and thoughtful discussion.

The end of life is relational—in physical terms, the end of relationships. We all will be, and should be, involved in discussions, both public and private, of such relationships at many different levels. The lecturers and commentators in this series will, I hope, have contributed to your participation in those discussions.

1

The Ends of Life:
Body, Mind and the Human Spirit
in Political Captivity

Terry Waite, MBE
Former Archbishop of Canterbury's Envoy to the Middle East

Thank you, gentlemen, for your welcome. Thank you, ladies and gentlemen, for your welcome also. I assume that I'm being welcomed outside as well even though you're sitting on the floor. My apologies for that. It is a great pleasure for me to be here today and to address this very broad and wide subject.

As you have heard, my job really is, as someone quite eloquently put it yesterday, to lay the table, to perhaps point to one or two issues, the majority of which I have had to face in my own experience, which will be broadened out, analyzed and investigated in much greater detail in the lectures to follow this particular one.

Before embarking though, two things. First, let me say that I am conscious of the fact that I am speaking here today in Canada at a time when there are two Canadians held hostage. I am also conscious of the fact that a fellow countryman of mine is also held at this time along with them. I am sure that I reflect your view if I say publicly that at this time our thoughts and prayers are with the families of those who wait at this very difficult time for them.

It is one thing to be taken hostage. It is also exceptionally difficult to be a family member and to wait and hope and to keep that waiting and the hoping going across the years. But I say to the families, maintain hope. It was four years before my own wife had any news that I was alive and she maintained hope with the children across that period of time, a difficult thing to do.

1

The second thing I'd like to say is that as my subject tonight is a serious subject, let me begin with a light-hearted story. When I came out of captivity I was invited to speak on many platforms and to travel here, there and everywhere, and I refused virtually everything because I needed time to readjust to the world as it had changed. I needed time to get to know my family again. When I was captured, my son was 14 years of age. When I returned, five years later, he was a young man and I hardly recognized him. So I needed time.

But I did agree to one invitation and that was to start the London Marathon. Not that I had any intention to run in the London Marathon, but I agreed for two reasons. The first reason being that the London Marathon begins in Greenwich Park, which is just behind our house in South East London, Blackheath. So it was a local event. And secondly, by going to the Marathon and starting the runners on their way I'd receive a considerable sum of money, which I could give to a local charity of my choice. And as the local school needed help, here was a very quick and easy way to make sure they got help.

On the morning of the Marathon, I set off to walk across the green to the starting point. As I was walking across the heath, I saw a small family sitting there—a lady with two small children—and I stopped to speak with them. I exchanged a few words, went on my way, started the Marathon, came home and forgot about the whole experience.

The next week there was a letter in the post and it was from the lady to whom I had spoken that particular morning and she wrote as follows. She said, "Mr. Waite, on the morning of the Marathon, I was sitting with my two children, Jamie, aged six, and Janice, aged four. As you were coming across the heath Jamie looked up and said, 'Oh, look. There's Terry Waite. He was a hostage for five years.' And to our surprise," she said, "you came across and you spoke with us. Did you notice little Janice, aged four, staring at you? When you went away," wrote the lady, "Janice turned to me and said, 'Mummy, is it true, was that man really an ostrich for five years?'"

It is said that ostriches have a tendency to bury their heads in the sand, and when one looks at some of the issues that face us in this lecture series, I wouldn't blame anyone for wishing to bury their head in the sand and to perhaps try and avoid them. But they are issues that need to be taken seriously and that need to be debated publicly and, as I understand it, this lecture series is intended to stimulate public thought and debate around critical issues that face us in our time.

Before moving directly into my personal story of captivity, let me begin simply three weeks ago. Three weeks ago I was in Australia and I was in the mountains—the Flinders Mountains—and I went in the company of two people: one, a geologist who had an intimate knowledge of that region and who could explain in terms that a layman such as myself could understand something about the unique geographical and geological features of that region, and the other, an astronomer.

The night sky in that part of Australia is remarkable to see. You are in a remote region. You have no light pollution and you have absolute clarity. And if you go to the little telescope at the top of one of the mountains (I say "little," it is in fact a very advanced telescope) and you look at the Milky Way you can see the individual stars with surprising definition and clarity.

As I walked that part of the countryside and listened to the formation of the rocks and the history described to me by the geologist, and I looked at the heavens, I was struck with a sense of awe and wonder. There, miles and miles away from a city, miles and miles away from civilization as we know it, there in the midst of the Flinders Mountains I was alone with just a few companions and struck with a sense of awe and mystery. What a remarkable universe in which we live and what a mysterious place we live in. It's that sort of feeling that, in fact, provides inspiration for what we begin to call spirituality. The recognition that there is more to life than is often credited by modern industrial society. There is more to life than simply producing, manufacturing, gaining. All important, of course, but life extends beyond that and at the root there lies mystery and awe and wonder.

Spiritual truth is one form of truth. Scientific truth is another form of truth. One does not cancel out the other. And spiritual truth is equally as valid as scientific truth, although operating in a different framework. It is the sense of awe and mystery that leads us through to developing the frameworks that in some way enable us to interpret that mystery. This is the way in which religious movements begin and develop in different

3

professions and different religions. And they begin, as the religious traditions develop, to develop their own codes, their own ways of behaving.

You might say that within religious traditions there are two streams: on the one hand, the stream of love and compassion and on, the other hand, the stream of power and control. And they coexist. And at times sometimes the power and control and the admonition seems to dominate as you can see when you read the books of the Old Testament, or a Torah, and at other times the voice of compassion comes through strongly.

The great Rabbi Hillel, who was a teacher of the law, was once asked to perform one of those religious tricks, one might say. He was asked if he could recite the whole of the Torah, the whole of the law, while standing on one foot. He said he would do it easily and he said to his questioner, "Do not do anything to your neighbour that is hateful to you. And that is the law, go and learn." And then he placed his foot firmly on the ground again. It took him just a few moments to sum up the essence of the Torah, the law, as expounded in the Old Testament and as developed by Jesus, who said memorably, "Love your neighbour as yourself." But he summed it up in that way, in that pithy way, that is, the law and the prophets.

And there you have it: at the heart of spirituality, at the heart of any organization, any group that calls itself religious, there needs to be that constant stream of love and compassion. Spirituality is not and should not be confined, and definitely is not confined, to religious groupings. It is quite possible, and indeed highly desirable and at times very evident, that people who would not, in fact, claim any particular religious leaning or claim any allegiance to any particular religious grouping, nevertheless, in their own lives have profound respect for spirituality. There are many people who are totally dissatisfied with the lack of spirituality in secular society and would long to see spiritual values more clearly expressed in and through secular society.

It is amazing to say this—to have to say this—that love and compassion have the power to change. Take, for example, going back to the old days—the might of the pharaohs compared to the position of Moses, or the power of Rome compared to the simple message of Christ. Or to bring it up to date, the mighty power of the apartheid regime in South Africa and the simple, honest, loving witness of a person such as Desmond Tutu: the power of compassion and love.

I have often used this illustration when I said, with all due respect to those who are dead, and in particular with reference to the situation in the Middle East between the Israelis and the Palestinians, it is such a pity in that situation that up to this point the gun-toting image of someone such as the late President Arafat was the image that was propagated: the image of warfare. Yes, one could understand why people could find themselves totally frustrated and believing that change can be brought about by warfare. But compare that image to the image that was propagated by such people as Desmond Tutu. I have often stayed with him in South Africa and seen the pressure to which he was subject, seen the attempts made to actually destroy him, and he has always responded out of love and compassion that is based on his deep spirituality. And eventually, in that situation, the situation was turned without undue violence and with a minimum loss of life.

End view is mentioned tonight in the lecture, and does the attitude shape our action now—undoubtedly it does. Just the other day, I was lecturing at a university in the United States of America. I had been asked to compare two sets of martyrs. On the one hand, Christian martyrs, and on the other hand, so-called contemporary martyrs, suicide bombers. Points of similarity and points of difference.

I suppose to take the point of similarity first of all, both strongly believed, and strongly believe, in the case of suicide bombers today, that their action will gain them immediate entry into paradise in their own terms. There is one point of linkage. But the points of difference are enormous. It was always considered wrong in Christian tradition for individuals to commit suicide. Certainly, individuals who do that should be viewed with the deepest compassion, but it was not considered to be appropriate. Martyrs were not committing suicide; they were taken to martyrdom. It was always considered wrong to engage in murder and to involve others in your death, something which suicide bombers do. They involve other people in their martyrdom, so-called. So the differences are vast, but the end shapes the way in which people behave.

5

It is at this point I want to come down in much more concrete terms to my own experience. As you know, I worked for a number of years with the Archbishop of Canterbury. I became involved with seeking the release of hostages in difference situations: in Iran, in Libya and in Beirut. My way of negotiating was a way that doesn't work in every situation, but that works in certain situations and it was a way that is full of risk and difficulty. It was, first of all, to seek a face-to-face meeting with hostage-takers.

Now immediately you can see the difficulty of that because you are dealing with people who are highly volatile. You are dealing with people who are very nervous. You are dealing with people who have the capacity to take you at any moment and, therefore, you are in a very vulnerable position. It was successful to work in that way in Iran and in Libya and, in part, in Beirut.

My strategy was, first of all, to seek a meeting with people and, secondly, to attempt to build a relationship of trust. That means if you're going to build a relationship of trust with people from a different culture, you need to be able to sit with them and to listen and to try to understand them. Why is it that they are behaving as they are behaving—to try and get to the real reason behind the stereotyping. And if you can begin to get to that point, to build trust, to get to the root issue and to try and find a way of resolving the issue in a way that enables parties to the problem to walk away, in so far as it is possible, with their dignity intact. That way of working, as I said, was successful on a number of occasions. And it was partially successful in Lebanon. It failed for reasons that I shall explain in a second.

I met with the captors of the British hostages—western hostages, not just British hostages, in Beirut under extremely tense and difficult circumstances. They came to me with their demands. Their demands were very simple. They had blood relatives who were being held under a variety of terrorist charges in Kuwait and they wanted me to look into that problem. They said that these men who were their relatives were being held in an underground prison, they were being badly treated, they had no communication with their families and, altogether, it was a situation that was, in their opinion, totally impossible.

That gave me an opportunity to move in. I said that I could not engage in activity that would breach the law, that I would not be prepared to breach the law. But it gave me an opportunity as a humanitarian to say that I believe that all people who are detained legally ought to be treated fairly and properly under the law and, therefore, it gives me an opportunity to look into that. I went away and two hostages, at that point, were released: Father Martin Jenco, a Roman Catholic priest, and the Reverend Benjamin Weir, a Presbyterian minister. It was significant that two church people were released. It was said to me that they were being released as a sign to the church to keep up its activity in this respect.

I came back to the United Kingdom from Lebanon and I began to try and get into Kuwait. I had no success whatsoever. I could not understand why my own government or why the government of the United States could not give me support, political support, simply to get into Kuwait and look at this problem in the way that I said that I would try and do so. I was able to get letters through from their families. That was all. And then, it became horribly clear.

Whenever hostages from the United States of American were released, they went to Wiesbaden in Germany—Wiesbaden being a military base and a hospital base. They went there for a medical check-up, they went to meet with their families and they also had a political debriefing given by the CIA. When Father Martin Jenco and the Reverend Benjamin Weir were released, they went to Wiesbaden.

I went to Wiesbaden. I met with them there. I met with their families. I picked up whatever information I could about the other hostages.

A man by the name of David Jacobsen was released, an American. And David went to Wiesbaden. And David was convinced that I had obtained his release. I couldn't understand what I had done. I had totally failed to get into Kuwait, as I said, and then, as I said, it became horribly clear. One day in Wiesbaden I was sitting in a small room when someone came in and said, "Have you heard the news?" And I said, "What news?" They said there's a story that David Jacobsen has been released as a result of arms dealing. And at that point my heart sank. The name of Colonel Oliver North was mentioned and my heart sank

7

further. This was the beginning of what was to become known as the Iran–Contra Affair, which, in a nutshell was this: at the time Iran was fighting the Iran–Iraq war and it was important for Iran to have victory in that war. Iran was also supporting Hizbullah in Lebanon, with money, with arms, and with personnel and was seeking to propagate Islamic fundamentalism through Lebanon, through the Middle East. Colonel Oliver North, acting on behalf of others in the United States, made an approach through Iran and said, "If you will pressure your clients, Hizbullah, in Lebanon to release hostages, we will supply you with arms." This deal took place. Weapons were supplied to Iran. Money was paid which went through Colonel North to be used to support Contras in Nicaragua in Central America and the whole deal was supposed to be totally secret until it broke in the press, and broke to the world for the first time, and to me for the first time.

When I heard this news about Lebanon in Wiesbaden, I went straight to a secure telephone. I dialled the White House and I asked to be put through to Colonel North. And I said, "What is this?" He said, "Oh, don't worry. It will pass in a few days." I knew it wouldn't. I came back to the United Kingdom with a very, very heavy heart indeed. Now there was a total political collapse because the whole story had broken and it looked as though I myself was implicated in arms dealing. Not only I myself, but it looked as though I had implicated my Archbishop and the church in arms dealings, something with which I could have no truck whatsoever.

This faced me with one of the most difficult decisions I have had to take in my life and this, in part, refers to our principal point of discussion tonight. If my ground had been purely political, at that point undoubtedly I would have walked away. It would have been the sensible thing to do. It would have been a wise thing to do. But my ground was not primarily political. My ground was certainly humanitarian, and I like to think that there were other values that I have that were operative in that situation.

But, on the other hand, if anyone stands on a public platform and tells you that their motives are totally altruistic, you are, in my opinion, entitled to be a little cynical because we all have mixed motives. There was pride certainly involved in that. My pride had been hurt. I had been wounded by this association, and there was also a determination to say, "I'm sorry, but I'm not going to be beaten in this particular way." I determined that I would go back. Many attempts were made to dissuade me and my Archbishop said, "Do not go under any circumstances." I said, "If you will not let me go, I'm afraid I shall have to resign and go back independently." I cannot blame my Archbishop for saying that. If it had been a member of my staff who wanted to go under such circumstances, I would have had to say, "I'm sorry, I cannot give you my blessing." Eventually, he agreed and I went back.

I remember leaving my home at four o'clock in the morning to get an early plane. There was deep snow on the ground. I didn't even say ... I didn't even wake my wife or children to say goodbye because I hoped I would be home in a matter of 14 days. As it was, it turned out to be 1,763 days. I got to the airport. I got into Beirut. I went around trying to pick up the threads of the problem. Meeting the Prime Minister; meeting Sheikh Fadlallah the spiritual leader of Hizbullah; trying to pick up the issues. Then one evening the telephone rang. It was my contact from Hizbullah, from the kidnappers. He said, "Will you come and meet us?" I said, "Of course. That is why I am here." He said, "Come tomorrow night, to the same place." The same place being where I always had the meetings with the kidnappers on many previous occasions, in a doctor's consulting room.

When I got there, I felt something was wrong. The phone rang. The doctor answered it. He said, "I'm sorry. I have to leave you. There's an urgent case at the hospital." I said, "Can't you wait a moment?" He said, "No, you must go. Close the door when you leave," and he went. And I remember distinctly to this day taking my shoes off and walking up and down his consulting room thinking should I stay, should I go? And I thought, "No, you have come so far, stay."

Then I heard the elevator come up. We were on the second floor. The door opened. It was my contact. What I'd expected was this: I expected that I would be taken downstairs to a car, because all these things had happened previously. I'd be blindfolded. I'd be taken to another car, change cars. We'd go to a safe house. I'd have a change of clothing and the examination. I'd probably wait three or four days with a blindfold and after three or four days, if all went well, I'd get to the hostages.

9

Everything happened as I had anticipated excepting the last bit. We went to a car, changed cars, went to a safe house, changed clothing, and so on. In three or four days, they came for me in the middle of the night. We went out into the night, into a van and across Beirut. We drove into an underground garage. Looking beneath my blindfold, as I got out of the van, there was a trapdoor in the floor. They told me to jump down. I jumped down, and was pushed across the room. A door closed behind me and when I took my blindfold off, I was in a tiled cell. At that point, my heart sank because I realized that these underground prisons were tiled because they're easier to clean after people had been knocked around. And I realized that I was no longer a negotiator.

Now the tables had been turned and I was a hostage myself. And I was angry. That was my reaction—anger. Anger at being betrayed, at having trust betrayed. Anger at allowing myself to be drawn into that situation. Anger with myself for taking such a risk.

Three things came to mind at that point, and I'm not sure where they came from, but they probably came from the values that I'd been shaped by across life. No regrets—don't regret what you've done. You cannot have done everything right. You certainly haven't. But don't regret because you will be demoralized. No self-pity—don't be sorry for yourself. There are so many people in worse situations. And no over-sentimentality.

Don't say to yourself, "Oh, if only." If only I had had longer holidays. If only I had spent more time with the children, with the family. You can't. The past has been lived. You live with yourself as you are now. You can't be reliving the past.

I was kept in the cell, chained by the hands and feet to the wall 23 hours and 50 minutes a day with 10 minutes for the bathroom. I was always in a dark room. If I was above ground, metal shutters were put in front of the windows so no natural light came in. I had no books or papers or anything of that kind for years. And no communication with anyone, no one to speak with—four years of solitary confinement.

In the first year, year one: the year of interrogation. That was accompanied by beating on the soles of the feet with cable in order to get me to say what I knew about Iran–Contra. That was what all the questions were about. It was one of those times in life when I was awfully grateful I could stand on the truth. Who could say that they have always told the truth? I certainly couldn't.

I regret the times when I haven't told the truth in the past but I couldn't say that all my life I'd been absolutely and totally truthful. There were times when I hadn't really known what truth is.

But this occasion was one of the times when I realized what a powerful ally truth can be if it's on your side. I could say in the face of my captivity that I know nothing about that. And it was morally strengthening to be able to stand on truth. When they beat me on the soles of the feet with cable I felt, of course, acute pain. I couldn't walk for a week after that. But I felt a sense of pity and a sense also, I admit, of revulsion against those who commit such acts on someone who was totally defenceless.

Here is a passing comment: I am totally appalled that today so-called civilized governments can even entertain the idea of subjecting individuals to torture. To me it is incredible that any civilized government could even entertain that idea. It is degrading to the person who commits torture. It is degrading to the society from which that person comes and it is humiliating and degrading for the victim.

One day they came into my cell and said, "You have five hours to live." Well, at that point I was so exhausted I lay on the floor and I fell asleep.

At times of extreme crisis, at times of extreme strain, there are mechanisms that the body has for giving us protection, and this is an interesting point to examine at a later stage when you discuss these issues. My body took over and allowed me to sleep and I slept for what I imagine was five hours. I was awakened by people coming into the cell. They undid my shackles and told me to stand. I was pushed into the next room. There were several people in there. They said, "Do you want anything?" I said, "Yes. I would like to write some letters to my family, to my wife, my children, my mother, my Archbishop." "You can write one letter." They gave me a pen and paper and, looking beneath the blindfold, I wrote this one composite letter.

Anything else? I'd experienced what I'd only read about in books. I was afraid. And because I was afraid, my throat went dry and I asked for water. Well, in fact, I asked for tea, being English. They brought me tea.

I wasn't afraid of death. Death is something that we shall all experience. There will be no exceptions, of course. We shall all experience it and, therefore, it seems to me to be totally pointless to be afraid of death. What I was afraid of was the way in which I would die, the means by which I would die, the very simple human point—Would it hurt when the bullet went through my head? That's what made me afraid. That simple human feeling.

But death itself, no. Did I know? Did I have visions? Did I imagine that I would go straight to glory? No, not at all. Did I have great sustaining visions? No, not at all. Death is a natural phenomenon. No, it was not something to be afraid of. But the means, yes.

And also the fact that I did not want to die under such circumstances, leaving my family to say, "How did he spend his last years? How was he?" That would have been an awful burden for them, not to know how I lived my last hours or last days or indeed last years. They said, "Anything else?" I said, "Yes. I would like to say a prayer." Very well, and I said the Lord's Prayer. Then they said, "Turn around," and I turned around and the gun was put to my head and they dropped it and said "Another time." That was the end of my interrogation. This was the end of the first year.

They said, "We're going to release you now. We believe you." And then some event took place in the outside world. First, I was moved to good accommodation for a week or ten days. I was very well looked after, prepared to go out, and then something went wrong. I think I know what it was, but I can't be sure, so I won't say, and I was put back into normal hostage accommodation for another four years, for three of which I was totally alone.

I had to learn this time how to survive under a situation of extremity. And what I determined to do was somehow taken in a journey. It is very depressing at times to be totally alone, totally isolated from companionship, stimulation, any form of stimulation from the outside. You are very much on your own. You see your skin go white because you have no natural light. You lose muscle tone because there's no exercise apart from limited exercise you can do on the end of a chain. I broke a tooth on a stone in the bread, an abscess developed and there was no medicine apart from an aspirin. My beard that had been black grew long and white. I remember thinking to myself, "My goodness, I'm growing old before my time. My body, my physical body, is disintegrating and deteriorating rather more quickly than I would hope." I wondered, when that was happening, would I begin to disintegrate mentally and spiritually?

Would the same process take place? And I thought, "No, I can have some degree of control over mental and spiritual process. And one of the things I have to do is to take an inner journey to get to know my own sense of my own self more completely." An inner journey where you face up to yourself—the light and dark of self—is not an easy journey to take.

One can easily become depressed by the negative side of character that one is inevitably going to come across; no matter who you are you're going to come across it. And when you're alone and there's no one to support you or to reassure you, you can quickly fall into depression. And one has to guard against that.

The other extreme is I have known people in captivity who have cut off all internal communications. They have cut off communications with everybody around them and all internal communication and they've fallen into deep psychosis. Somehow it's developing the ability to find your centre, to be self-centred in the best sense of that word, and to allow that centre to grow and to flourish and somehow not to lose hope and a belief can enable you to have hope.

I have religious belief, yes. But in that whole time, I can honestly say that I did not feel what many religious people claim to feel and that is a close presence of God, a comforting presence of God; I did not feel it. I would not allow myself to engage in extemporary prayer, the prayer where you make up your own words, and enter into a familiar relationship with God. I wouldn't allow that for the simple reason that if I were to do that, I would almost certainly have gone down the pathway of saying, "Oh, God, get me out of here." And that would have just have been a cop-out.

I had to face up to the fact that I had gone into that situation of my own volition. It was my choice. I understood the

13

dangers of that situation and, therefore, it was my responsibility to cope with that situation and it would be totally ridiculous just to pray in that childish way, "Oh, please get me out of here." The situation had to be faced by myself as truthfully, as honestly as it could be faced.

I was very fortunate that across life I had been a reader, that I had committed to memory poetry and prose, because in those years I could recollect that which I had remembered. Good language and good music both have the capacity to breathe a certain harmony into the soul. And what I needed and what I was able to find in those years was harmony, a greater degree of inner harmony, despite the external situation.

My prayer was not the extemporary prayer, "Oh God, get me out of this situation." Rather, I fell back on the regular use of language and I was grateful that I'd been brought up in a religious tradition that gave me regular use of good language, a calling to the church, for example, "Lighten our darkness, we beseech thee, O Lord; and by thy great mercy, defend us from all the perils and dangers of this night." A prayer, a calling to the church, that has great significance and meaning when you're sitting in the dark, which has harmony, which has balance, which has rhythm, which has poetry, which breathes a certain harmony into the soul. And that was my prayer.

But there was no feeling. I often think that many people make a mistake when it comes to religion and things at that level, thinking that because they do not feel good, therefore they have lost faith or religion has no value. That is not necessarily the case at all.

Toward the end of my captivity, I was moved to be with others because I became rather seriously ill with what turned out to be a bronchial infection. At that point, I could not lie down. I had to remain sitting up day and night. I could hardly get my breath. And it was at that point where I remember saying to myself, "Death would almost now be preferable to what is becoming a living death." And yet, at that point even, I did not wish to give up. I felt, no, something within me hung onto life, not only for myself but for the sake of those for whom I cared— my family, my wife, my children, those around me. I said, "No, I will not, at this point, give up."

14

When I was sitting against the wall in the night, gasping for breath, Terry Anderson, the American hostage, would simply lean across and extend himself as far as he could on the end of a chain. He didn't say anything. He just stayed with me and put his hand on mine.

It was at that point I realized that when you visit people who are at the edge of life, who are desperately ill, and you perhaps sometimes worry that you don't know what to say—it doesn't matter. It doesn't matter what you say. That isn't the point. The point is that there is another human being alongside you who, with compassion and understanding, will be with you. And again the values come through. The values of compassion and care and understanding, which lie at the heart, surely, of any religious tradition worth its soul and they're conveyed without words.

One reason I think that there are miracles in the New Testament is not because they are rather clever conjuring tricks, more that they are stories to show that there can be good outcomes when there is no rational reason to believe that there will be a good outcome. And there was no rational reason in this situation to believe there might be a good outcome from this experience, but there was.

I look back on that experience, certainly painful and difficult days, but days which taught me something of the importance of the fundamental values that I have been doing my best to explain tonight—of compassion, of care, love and respect. Not necessarily expressed in religious language, but expressed perhaps more eloquently in the way we are, the way we conduct ourselves, the way we walk this earth as human beings seeking fullness and completeness in ourselves, for ourselves and for others.

Yes, the world as we know very well, and as you will examine in the days to come, is a world full of suffering. And suffering will be with us until the end of time. It is no respecter of persons. Some people suffer much more than others and certainly through no fault of their own. And that too, suffering, the origins of suffering, the reasons for suffering, remain an unfathomable mystery and, yet, I think it is possible to say with confidence that suffering need not destroy.

If you approach it and face it and go through it, it can be turned and it can be creative, perhaps in ways that you do not understand yourself or will never understand. Certainly we don't have to look for it. It will find us in one way or another and it would be unhealthy to look for it. But it need not destroy.

To me, religion, belief, spirituality is about transformation. It is about enabling us to be transformed into individuals and communities that have love and compassion in their heart. It means having respect for other people regardless of culture, regardless of background. It means having respect for the earth along which we tread and for the environment that we help shape or destroy. It means all those things.

And all the values that I hold dear and that many religions attempt to enshrine, those values, there is absolutely no reason why they should not be—in fact, there is every reason why they ought to be—debated and exercised in and through the public realm. They are not the prerogative of religious organizations only. They belong to us all as human beings, but they are not easily attained.

Thank you very much.

2

The Ends of Life and Death:
Public Policy, Spirituality and the Law

Jocelyn Downie, MA, MLitt, LLB, LLM, SJD
Canada Research Chair in Health Law and Policy
Professor, Faculties of Law and Medicine, Dalhousie University

It is always a pleasure to have the opportunity to speak with people about an issue that I care deeply about. It is also a pleasure to be challenged to reflect on a familiar topic from a new perspective. While my previous work on end-of-life law and policy has been informed by my own spirituality and, I hope, a sensitivity to and respect for the spiritual beliefs and values of others, I have never so explicitly and directly reflected on "the ends of life and death—law, public policy, and spirituality." So I would like to thank the organizers of the Segelberg Lecture Series for inviting me to give this talk on this topic and all of you for being here today. So let's jump right in.

Euthanasia and assisted suicide—few words take us more immediately to the intersection of law and spirituality. Beliefs about the meaning of life and suffering; beliefs about the definition and determination of death; beliefs about the significance and legitimacy of autonomy and agency in relation to the timing and cause of death: all of these beliefs motivate positions on what the law should be. Not surprisingly, however, they do not seem to take us to a single position on which all can agree. Indeed, polarized positions are frequently justified through reference to various competing conceptions of human spirituality. But it is my hope that we will be able to talk today (and over the coming lectures in this series) about spirituality and end-of-life law and policy without polarization. I hope that we will be able to explore the law in this highly charged spiritual arena in a constructive fashion. And so, in this lecture, I will first define my terms and then describe the current legal status of various end-of-life practices in Canada, including the withholding and withdrawal of potentially life-sustaining treatment, the provision of potentially life-shortening symptom relief, assisted suicide and euthanasia. I will then reflect on the role of spirituality in debates about what the legal status of these practices should be. I will also offer a brief look at some of the arguments for the decriminalization of euthanasia and assisted suicide that I think are particularly important for conversations at the nexus of spirituality and end-of-life law and policy.[1] I very much look forward to the comments from the other panellists as well as the audience, both today and throughout the upcoming year.

TERMINOLOGY

Betraying immediately that I began my academic career in Philosophy, I first turn to defining my terms. This is critical if we are to understand one another and to have constructive conversations about these issues.

"Withholding of potentially life-sustaining treatment" is the failure to start treatment that has the potential to sustain the life of a person (for example, not providing cardiopulmonary resuscitation to a person having a heart attack).

"Withdrawal of potentially life-sustaining treatment" is the stopping of treatment that has the potential to sustain the life of a person (for example, removing a feeding tube from a person in a persistent vegetative state).

"Potentially life-shortening symptom relief" is pain/suffering control medication given in amounts that may, but are not certain to, shorten a person's life (for example, the ever-increasing levels of morphine necessary to control an individual's pain from terminal cancer where the morphine is known to potentially depress respiration even to the point of causing death, but it is not known precisely how much is too much as the levels are slowly increased).

---

[1] Apart from the sections on spirituality, this text is largely taken directly from my book *Dying Justice: A Case for Decriminalizing Euthanasia and Assisted Suicide in Canada* (University of Toronto Press, 2004) [*Dying Justice*]. Portions have been changed to reflect changes in the law or available empirical evidence as between the date of the publication of *Dying Justice*, the time of the lecture and the date of publication of this volume.

The Ends of Life and Death:
Public Policy, Spirituality and the Law

"Assisted suicide" is the act of intentionally killing oneself with the assistance (that is, the provision of knowledge and/or means) of another person (for example, a person is bedridden with ALS—also known as Lou Gehrig's disease, her sister brings her a lethal dose of a barbiturate ground up in a glass of orange juice, and the person drinks it through a straw).

"Euthanasia" is an act undertaken by one person with the intention of ending the life of another person, to relieve that person's suffering, where that act is the cause of death (for example, a person is bedridden with ALS and her physician gives her a lethal injection of potassium chloride).

That first set of definitions was easy for me; I've been working with these terms for a number of years now. However, there is another key term that remains to be defined for the purposes of today's talk—"spirituality". I must confess that when I agreed to give this talk, I naively thought that the challenge posed for me by the organizers was to reflect on end-of-life law and policy and its relationship to spirituality. I thought the challenge would be in reflecting on the relationship. Little did I realize that I would be immediately stumped by the challenge of defining the term. No simple and satisfying definition is to be found in the *Oxford English Dictionary* (or a Canadian one or indeed any other dictionary). I would hazard a guess that, if a condition of entry today had been that each person submit a written definition of "spirituality", I would now have a hundred definitions (and a few of you might have given up in exasperation at the project and gone home already). But having agreed to give the talk, I couldn't simply give up. So after wandering through dictionaries and Internet sites and conversations with patient friends and family, I can offer the following quasi-definition, with the caveat that this is simply for the purposes of us having a common language for this afternoon.

> *"Spirituality"*—what it is not:
> * not the same thing as religion
> * not the opposite of atheism or humanism

> *"Spirituality"*—what it is:

- "big questions of metaphysics, meaning, existence"[2]
- "deepest aspects of reality, values, morals and meanings"[3]

And so, with my terms somewhat defined, I turn now to a description of what the law is with respect to the ends of life and death.

Withholding and withdrawal of potentially life-sustaining treatment

It is clear that, under Canadian law, health care professionals must respect refusals of treatment from competent adults (either direct refusals or refusals through valid advance directives[4]). The Supreme Court of Canada has made strong statements to this effect: Canadian courts have recognized a common law right of patients to refuse consent to medical treatment, or to demand that treatment, once commenced, be withdrawn or discontinued. This right has been specifically recognized to exist even if the withdrawal from or refusal of treatment may result in death.[5]

Potentially life-shortening symptom relief

Turning now to potentially life-shortening symptom relief, recall that this is the ever-increasing levels of medication that may but are not certain to shorten life. The question is, could someone who provides potentially life-shortening symptom relief find themselves charged with criminal negligence causing death (i.e., culpable homicide)? No case directly on point has reached the Supreme Court of Canada. However, there are some comments on point in the assisted suicide case involving Sue Rodriguez (Canada's most famous assisted suicide case

---

[2] http://coachingcircles.com/Spirituality--non-religious--Coaching
[3] *Ibid.*
[4] Advance directives are legal instruments through which competent individuals set out what decisions are to be made (instruction directives, colloquially known as living wills) or who is to make decisions on their behalf (proxy directives) in the event that they become incompetent.
[5] *Rodriguez v. British Columbia (Attorney General)*, [1993] 3 S.C.R. 519 at 156, quoting from *Ciarlariello* v. *Schacter*, [1993] 2 S.C.R. 119, *Nancy B. v. Hôtel-Dieu de Québec* (1992), 86 D.L.R. (4th) 385 (Que. S.C.); and *Malette v. Shulman* (1990), 72 O.R. (2d) 417.

about which I will say more in the next section). For the majority in *Rodriguez*, the late Justice Sopinka wrote:

> The administration of drugs designed for pain control in dosages which the physician knows will hasten death constitutes active contribution to death by any standard. However, the distinction drawn here is one based upon intention—in the case of palliative care the intention is to ease pain, which has the effect of hastening death, while in the case of assisted suicide, the intention is undeniably to cause death…. In my view, distinctions based upon intent are important, and in fact form the basis of our criminal law. While factually the distinction may, at times, be difficult to draw, legally it is clear.[6]

It can be argued, on the basis of this, that the provision of potentially life-shortening symptom relief is legal if the intention is to ease pain.

Assisted suicide

In contrast, assisted suicide is, quite clearly, illegal in Canada. Section 241(b) of the *Criminal Code* prohibits aiding or abetting a person to commit suicide (although, I should emphasize that suicide itself is no longer illegal). Sue Rodriguez, a woman suffering from ALS, challenged the constitutionality of this section of the *Code*. The Supreme Court of Canada upheld it (in an extraordinarily close 5:4 decision).

However, despite the illegality of assisted suicide, it is clear that it is happening in Canada. Twenty other cases are known to have reached the attention of the authorities in Canada.[7] In three, no charges were laid.[8] In two, charges were

---

[6] *Rodriguez, Ibid.* at 172.
[7] Eerkiyoot and Ishaka (1949), Amah, Avinga, and Nangmalik (1963), Lois Wilson (1985), David Lewis (1990), Sue Rodriguez (1993), Mary Jane Fogarty (1995), Maurice Genereux (1996), Bert Doerksen (1997), Wayne Hussey (2000), Richard Trites and Michael Breau (2001), Julianna Zsiros (2003), Evelyn Martens (2002), Marielle Houle (2004), Ramesh Sharma (2006) described and referenced online at Right to Die Society of Canada, online: www.righttodie.ca/assistedsuicides-canada.htm; Stephan Dufour (2007) "Quebec man accused of assisting uncle's suicide wants trial by jury" CBC News (July 18, 2007), online:

stayed or dropped.[9] In three, the accused were found not guilty.[10] There have been 11 convictions (guilty pleas or verdicts) but, of these, seven resulted in suspended sentences or probation.[11] So only three resulted in jail time being served.[12] The penalty in one remains unknown and one case remains outstanding.[13] The point of generating this flurry of numbers is to emphasize the fact that there have been no jail terms for individuals charged in the cases where the facts were the sort that proponents of decriminalization support (i.e., competent individuals suffering greatly and requesting assistance).

There is also some evidence that assisted suicide is happening in Canada and simply not reaching the criminal justice system. Russel Ogden conducted a study in the HIV/AIDS community in British Columbia between 1980 and 1993 and testified before the Senate Committee on Euthanasia and Assisted Suicide: "I learned of 34 cases of assisted suicide and euthanasia amongst the AIDS population [in BC]. I also learned of other deaths outside of the AIDS population, but did not include those in my data. I have learned of many more deaths amongst patients with ALS, cancer and AIDS since the publication of these findings."

More recently, Ogden has written about 19 helium bag–assisted suicide cases known to the BC coroner since 1999.[14] He has also noted that he has evidence of over 100 other helium-

<http://www.cbc.ca/canada/montreal/story/2007/07/18/qc-almaassistedsuicide0718.html>; and Elizabeth Jeannette MacDonald (2007), "No charges in assisted suicide case" CBC News (July 03, 2007), online: <http://www.cbc.ca/canada/nova-scotia/story/2007/07/03/rcmp-macdonald.html>.

[8] Lewis, Rodriguez, MacDonald, *supra* note 7.
[9] Doerksen, Breau, *supra* note 7.
[10] Ishakak, Hussey, Martens, *supra* note 7.
[11] Amah, Avinga, Nangmelik, Fogarty, Zsiros, Houle, Trites, *supra* note 7.
[12] Eerkiyoot, Genereux, Wilson, *supra* note 7.
[13] Sharma, Dufour, *supra* note 7.
[14] "Helium in an 'exit bag' new choice for suicide" (December 8, 2007), online: Vancouver Sun
<http://www.canada.com/vancouversun/news/story.html?id=ce4139ae-d635-4030-ac92-a7b7d6fab09d>

related deaths in North America between 1999 and 2002 that were not reported to the authorities.[15]

A 1995 study conducted in Manitoba found that of the physicians who responded to the survey, 15% had facilitated a patient's request to shorten life by assisted suicide or euthanasia[16] —this is fairly described as an underestimate as the researchers were asking physicians to self-report on criminal activity.

Thus, although clearly prohibited by law, assisted suicide is happening but it is, on the whole, not being prosecuted and, where prosecuted and convictions obtained, very little if any jail time is being served. The law on the books is clearly prohibitive. However, the law on the street appears to be somewhat tolerant (albeit very unevenly). In other words, assisted suicide is illegal but practiced and, to a certain extent, countenanced.

Euthanasia

Euthanasia, like assisted suicide, is quite clearly illegal in Canada. It is prohibited by s.229 of the *Criminal Code* and consent does not provide a defence.[17] First-degree murder (which euthanasia is under the current law) carries with it a mandatory minimum life sentence with no possibility of parole for 25 years.[18] Clearly, this is a serious prohibition.

That said, however, a review of the cases involving or allegedly involving euthanasia sends a very different message. There have been 18 cases in which charges were laid against individuals.[19] One individual ran away to Israel,[20] one was not

---

15 *Ibid.*
16 N. Searles, "Silence Doesn't Obliterate the Truth: A Manitoba Survey on Physician Assisted Suicide and Euthanasia" (1996) 4 Health L. Rev. 9. [Manitoba].
17 *Criminal Code*, R.S.C. 1985, c. C-46.
18 *Ibid.*
19 Victor and Dorothy Ramberg (1941), George Davis (1942), Ron Brown (1978), Nachum Gal (1982), Robert Cashin (1994), Bruno Bergeron (1985), Alberto de la Rocha (1991), Scott Mataya (1991), Cheryl Myers and Michael Power (1993), Robert Latimer (1993), Jean Brush (1994), Danielle Blais (1996), Nancy Morrison (1997), Herbert Lerner (2000), Alain Quimper (2002), Tony Jaworski (2004) described and referenced online at Right to Die Society of Canada, online: www.righttodie.ca/assistedsuicides-canada.htm.
20 Gal, *supra* note 19.

taken past the preliminary hearing,[21] three were acquitted,[22] seven were convicted with suspended sentences (plea bargains from murder to administration of a noxious substance or manslaughter),[23] four were convicted on lesser charges (manslaughter or administration of a noxious substance) one with two years probation,[24] one with three years probation,[25] one with two years in jail[26] and one with five years in jail.[27] Two were convicted for murder, both with life sentences.[28] So, to turn this flurry of numbers into a single snowball—18 cases with only four jail terms.

These numbers stand in stark contrast to the strong prohibition of euthanasia found in the *Criminal Code*. Again, there appears to be a disconnect between the law on the books and the law on the street.

What spiritual issues are engaged

From this description of what the law *is* with respect to end of life in Canada, I turn now to a brief discussion of the spiritual issues that are engaged when questions are asked about what the law *should be* with respect to end of life.

It is very difficult to find jokes to liven up a talk on euthanasia. Fortunately, the inclusion of spirituality in this talk provides me with an opportunity to introduce a touch of levity here. If you look on the Internet for the "big questions of metaphysics, meaning, existence" (taking the quasi-definition of spirituality I offered earlier,) you find a number of more or less illuminating bumper stickers:

---

[21] *R.* v. *Morrison,* [1998] N.S.J. No. 75, online: QL (NSJ).

[22] Ramberg, Ramberg, Davis, *supra* note 19.

[23] Bergeron and Blais, *supra* note 19, *R.* v. *Mataya* (unreported Ontario Court of Justice (General Division), 24 Aug. 1992 Wren J. without a jury); *R.* v. *de la Rocha* (1993), Timmins, (Ont. Ct. (Gen. Div.)); *R.* v. *Myers and Power* (23 Dec. 1994), Halifax, (N.S.S.C.).; *R.* v. *Brush* (2 March 1995) Toronto (Ont. Ct. J. (Prov. Div.)).

[24] Cashin, *supra* note 19.

[25] Jaworski, *supra* note 19.

[26] Brown, *supra* note 19.

[27] Lerner, *supra* note 19.

[28] Quimper, *supra* note 19, and *R.* v. *Latimer,* [2001] 1 S.C.R. 3, 193 D.L.R. (4th) 577 (S.C.C.

- "hello. anybody out there?"[29]
- in the design style of the famous "got milk?" ads: "got purpose?"[30]
- beside a photo of Johnny Depp in *Pirates of the Caribbean*: "But why is the rum gone?"[31]

And my personal favourite:

- "what if the *hokey pokey* really *is* what it's all about?"[32]

Cast less as slogans, the spiritual issues engaged by end-of-life law and policy include, but of course are not limited to:

- when does life end?
- what follows life?
- what is the value of life without consciousness?
- what is the value of life without the capacity to engage with others?
- when is a life no longer worth living?
- when can we allow death to occur?
- when can we cause death?
- what is the meaning/value of suffering..., dignity..., life..., autonomy..., and agency?

We must reflect on these and other questions if we want to figure out ... what we think about assisted death... whether we would seek assisted suicide or euthanasia for ourselves... and whether we would provide assistance with suicide or euthanasia to someone else (e.g., a loved one or, for health care professionals, a patient).

Respectful engagement in a spiritually charged arena

I should note here that I do not see how we can engage in discussions of law and policy about end-of-life issues without reflecting on spirituality. The answers to the questions just mentioned are at the heart of justifications for positions in this arena. And these questions, while they are not all there is to

---

[29] www.bumperart.com
[30] www.cafepress.com
[31] *Ibid.*
[32] *Ibid.*

spirituality, are surely at the heart of it for many people. Unfortunately, however, too often discussions of end-of-life law and policy devolve into sloganeering, shouting matches and vitriolic *ad hominems*. But this is not necessary. And it is certainly not desirable or productive. And so I propose the following: that is, if we are to have respectful engagement in this spiritually charged arena, we must take at least the following steps:

1. Reflect on our own beliefs and values
2. Gather and critically assess relevant information
3. Ensure consistency of our positions across issues
4. Seek to understand what beliefs and values are motivating the positions of others
5. Challenge the positions of others (and be open to challenge) about inconsistencies, invalid arguments, factual errors...
6. Respect remaining differences that survive the challenges

What the law should be

Following on the six steps outlined above, I would like to offer some reflections on the current status of end-of-life law and policy. In particular, I would like to suggest that what I have reviewed here today illustrates the need for law reform.

First, I would argue that the approach taken to assisted suicide and euthanasia should be harmonized:

~ The euthanasia cases to date reveal the lack of a standard response across the country. It is possible that a health care provider in Nova Scotia might perform exactly the same act as a health care provider in Alberta and be tried for murder here and be allowed to plead guilty to the administration of a noxious substance there. This seems manifestly unfair.

~ Either we believe that voluntary euthanasia deserves a punishment less than at least 25 years in jail (in which case we should amend the *Criminal Code* to reflect that) or we believe that it deserves at least 25 years in jail (in which case we should stop this pattern of accepting pleas to manslaughter and administration of a noxious substance). The *status quo* seems hypocritical.

Second, I would argue that the approach taken to assisted suicide and euthanasia should be less restrictive:

~ At the very least, the mandatory minimum life sentence should not apply to euthanasia. Such a penalty, I would argue, does not serve the objectives of punishment (i.e., deterrence, protection, rehabilitation and one I am not so keen on, retribution). It is more severe than need be for deterrence, and those who perform euthanasia are not a danger to society that can only be guarded against by putting them behind bars for 25 years, and rehabilitation is arguably the least likely result of 25 years in prison for an individual who commits euthanasia.

~ More controversially, I would also argue that we should decriminalize assisted suicide and euthanasia and then apply a rigorous regulatory regime to these activities.

It is here that I most clearly return to the fifth step in what I described earlier as respectful engagement: "Challenge positions of others about inconsistencies, invalid arguments, factual errors,..." If I had a few hours with you, I would enjoy canvassing all of the arguments that I think need to be made here to make a comprehensive case for the decriminalization of euthanasia and assisted suicide. But, rest assured I will not be keeping you here for hours and so I will go over just those arguments that I think are particularly important for conversations at the nexus of spirituality and end-of-life law and policy. Specifically, I will discuss distinctions between kinds of assisted death as well as arguments based on claims about sanctity of life, suffering as a source of meaning, slippery slopes and palliative care.

An unsustainable distinction

My first argument is that it is not possible to justify the current legal distinction—on the one hand the law permits the withholding and withdrawal of life-sustaining treatment and the provision of potentially life-shortening symptom relief while, on the other hand, it prohibits assisted suicide and euthanasia.

Permitted	Prohibited
Withholding	Assisted suicide
Withdrawal	Euthanasia
Symptom relief	

I will argue that if one is prepared to be permissive on the left of the chart, then I believe that one is logically compelled to be permissive on the right. Canadian law *does* permit the withholding and withdrawal of potentially life-sustaining treatment and the provision of potentially life-shortening symptom relief. Therefore, Canadian law *should* permit assisted suicide and euthanasia. In order to sustain this argument, I must demonstrate why a range of justifications offered in support of this distinction do not do the work expected of them, specifically, acts/omissions, natural/unnatural death and motive of ending suffering vs. ending life.

NATURE OF CONDUCT *act vs. omission*
    The acts/omissions distinction argument generally takes the following form:

1. to omit to save a life is acceptable whereas to act to end life is unacceptable;
2. the withholding and withdrawal of potentially life-sustaining treatment are omissions, but assisted suicide and euthanasia are acts;
3. therefore, the withholding and withdrawal of potentially life-sustaining treatment are acceptable but assisted suicide and voluntary euthanasia are not.

There are at least two bases on which to lay a claim that the acts/omissions distinction is not a sustainable distinction upon which to ground public policy with respect to assisted death. First, the withdrawal of potentially life-sustaining treatment is as much an act as assisted suicide and euthanasia are acts. Second, there is no moral significance to the distinction between acts and omissions. I will consider each of these in turn.
    First, let us consider my claim that the withdrawal of potentially life-sustaining treatment is an act. In the context of assisted death, something is an act when you *do* something knowing that but for your action the person would not die. Something is an omission when you *do not do* something knowing that but for your omission the person would not die. When you withhold a necessary blood transfusion you are *not doing* something. Therefore, withholding treatment is an omission. When you withdraw a respirator you are *doing* something. Therefore,

28

withdrawing treatment is an act. When you give ever-increasing levels of morphine, you are *doing* something. Symptom relief is an act. When you give a person a lethal injection you are *doing* something. Therefore, euthanasia is an act. Therefore, it cannot be concluded that withholding and withdrawal are acceptable because they are omissions, and assisted suicide and euthanasia are unacceptable because they are acts. Withholding is an omission, while withdrawal, symptom relief, assisted suicide and euthanasia are acts.

Second, consider my claim that there is no moral significance to the acts/omissions distinction. Consider the following example (which is a modification of James Rachels' famous example[33]). Smith stands to gain a large inheritance if anything should happen to his young cousin Jones. Jones is in hospital following a car accident. He is on a respirator, but is expected to recover fully. In the first scenario, Smith enters the hospital room surreptitiously and disconnects the respirator. In the second scenario, Smith is visiting his cousin and simply watches as Jones has a violent seizure and accidentally disconnects the power supply to the respirator. In both scenarios, Jones dies. Although in scenario one Smith acts and in scenario two he omits to act, both the act and the omission are reprehensible, but the acts/omissions distinction plays no role in Smith's culpability.

A number of arguments have been made in response to the conclusion that there is no morally significant distinction between acts and omissions. In the space of this presentation, I cannot review and rebut all of these arguments. However, I can identify a fatal flaw shared by these arguments. That is, they all end up relying upon a feature *in addition to* the acts/omissions feature. The feature itself may vary between the arguments (it might be intentionality, causation or probability of death), but the addition of a feature is shared. The addition of a feature means that there is something other than the acts/omissions distinction itself that is critical. For example, it might be argued in response to these examples that in both Smith is culpable, but that while in the second case Smith is bad, in the first he is worse. The acts/omissions distinction therefore retains moral signifi-

---

[33] J. Rachels, "Euthanasia, Killing, and Letting Die," in J. Ladd, ed., *Ethical Issues Relating to Life and Death* (New York: Oxford University Press, 1979) at 154.

cance. However, this response only shows that, if anything, the acts/omissions distinction is relevant to relative culpability. It does not establish that the distinction distinguishes morally acceptable from morally unacceptable conduct. Something more is needed. Activity alone does not make conduct morally wrong (e.g., the withdrawal of life-sustaining treatment). Inactivity alone does not make conduct morally right (e.g., watching). Thus, the acts/omissions distinction alone does not do the work desired of it. An additional element is required. Potential additional elements will be considered, and rejected, in the next sections of this presentation (e.g., cause of death and the intention to end life).

CAUSE OF DEATH *disease/"natural" vs. action/"unnatural"*
    Another argument frequently made is that when a health care provider withholds or withdraws treatment, the disease kills the patient whereas when a health care provider performs euthanasia, a drug kills the patient. Framed another way, in the former, death results from "natural causes" whereas in the latter, it results from "unnatural causes". So, for example, Yale Kamisar argues, "In letting die, the cause of death is seen as the underlying disease process or trauma. In assisted suicide/euthanasia, the cause of death is seen as the inherently lethal action itself."[34]
    However, this natural/unnatural or disease/action distinction does not map onto the legal distinction with the withholding and withdrawal of potentially life-sustaining treatment on the one side and assisted suicide and euthanasia on the other.
    As with assisted suicide and euthanasia, an "unnatural cause" (the removal of a respirator) rather than a "natural cause" (the underlying disease) can cause death in a case involving withdrawal of potentially life-sustaining treatment. An example should help to illustrate this point. Consider someone who had polio as a child and requires a respirator for daily living. If a thief removed the respirator from that person, few would say that the polio killed the person or that the person died of natural causes. Most, if not all, would say that the removal of the respirator killed the person and the person died of unnatural causes. Consider also a person with a pacemaker. Someone intentionally

[34] Y Kamisar, "Against Assisted Suicide – Even a Very Limited Form" (1995) U. Det. Mercy L. Rev. 735.

releases a strong electromagnetic pulse when she enters a room, the pulse causes her pacemaker to stop working and she dies. Did she die of natural causes? Was the agent of her death the underlying heart disease that required that she have a pacemaker or was it the electromagnetic pulse? Most, if not all, would say that the pulse killed the woman and that she died of unnatural causes and, yet, this is ultimately an example of withdrawal of treatment.

INTENTION *to end life vs. to alleviate suffering*

Intention is frequently cited in an attempt to draw a distinction between the withholding and withdrawal of potentially life-sustaining treatment on the one hand and euthanasia on the other. It is argued that the intention of withholding and withdrawal is to alleviate suffering while the intention of assisted suicide and euthanasia is to end life. Hastening death with the intention of alleviating suffering is considered acceptable and hastening death with the intention of ending life is considered unacceptable. Therefore, it is argued, the withholding and withdrawal and symptom relief are acceptable and assisted suicide and euthanasia are not.

However, one must distinguish between two senses of intention: subjective foresight and motive/goal. Death is frequently a known consequence of the withholding and withdrawal of potentially life-sustaining treatment. Therefore, on the subjective foresight meaning of intention, the argument dissolves. Just as when a health care provider injects a lethal dose of potassium chloride, when a health care provider withdraws artificial hydration and nutrition, she knows that a consequence of that action will be death. The subjective foresight test can be met by categories of assisted death on either side of the line between withholding and withdrawal and symptom relief and assisted suicide and euthanasia.

Similarly, the motive/goal of all forms of assisted death is to alleviate suffering. Therefore, on this meaning of intention, the argument also dissolves. When a health care provider withdraws artificial hydration and nutrition, her motive is to alleviate suffering. When a health care provider injects a lethal dose of potassium chloride, her motive is to alleviate suffering. Again, the motive test can be met by categories of assisted death on either side of the current legal line.

It is here that the principle of double effect must be considered. On this principle, "it is sometimes permissible to bring about by oblique intention what one may not directly intend." However, this principle cannot ground a distinction between the categories of assisted death because it too captures some events on both sides of the line. Just as when a health care provider injects a lethal dose of potassium chloride, when he or she withdraws artificial hydration and nutrition at the request of a patient, there is no primary effect that excuses the secondary effect. There is no effect of alleviating suffering apart from the effect of ending life. Ending life is the means to ending the suffering. The intention to end life is direct rather than "oblique" and hence, on the principle of double effect, impermissible. And yet, the withdrawal of artificial hydration and nutrition from a patient is and ought to be legally permissible. Therefore, the principle of double effect cannot be used to ground the distinction between the withholding and withdrawal of potentially life-sustaining treatment on the one hand and assisted suicide and euthanasia on the other.

SANCTITY OF LIFE

Sanctity of life arguments can be divided into two categories: religious and secular. The religious arguments tend to be based on the view that life is sacred and on divine commandments (e.g., in Christianity, the Sixth Commandment, "Thou shalt not kill"). The secular argument tends to be based on deontological arguments positing a rule: Do not kill. This rule can be derived from a moral theory such as that set out by Immanuel Kant.[35] The secular argument is also frequently grounded in the following argument: the principle that "killing is wrong" is widely recognized as being a foundational principle in our society. Euthanasia and assisted suicide violate this principle; therefore, they ought not to be permitted.

With respect to the religious sanctity of life arguments, it should first be noted that not all religious groups in fact oppose

---

[35] I. Kant, *Foundations of the Metaphysics of Morals* (L.W. Beck trans.) (Indianapolis: Bobbs-Merrill Educational Publishing, 1980).

the decriminalization of assisted suicide and euthanasia. Not all religious groups accept the claim that the sanctity of life principle demands a prohibitive regime.[36] Second, while many Canadians believe in a Christian commandment, many others do not. The existence of a Christian commandment alone is neither necessary nor sufficient to ground a legal response.[37] It is not necessary—fishing without a licence is illegal even though it is not contrary to any religious principle. It is not sufficient—commandments prohibit adultery, taking the Lord's name in vain, and coveting a neighbour's house, but none of these activities are illegal in Canada.[38] While there is sometimes overlap between religious and legal principles, congruence is not universal. The mere fact that a particular religious group holds a particular belief is in itself neither a reason to keep it out of the law nor a reason to put it in the law. The religious principle of sanctity of life is therefore not grounds for prohibiting assisted suicide and euthanasia in Canada.[39]

With respect to the secular sanctity of life argument based on the view that "killing is wrong" is a foundational principle in our society, the following responses can be made. First, "killing is wrong" is not an absolute principle in our society. For example, self-defence is an absolute defence to a charge of murder.[40] Killing is permitted (indeed ordered) by the state in

---

[36] J. Childress, "Religious Viewpoint" in L.L. Emmanuel, ed., *Regulating How We Die: The Ethical, Medical and Legal Issues Surrounding Physician-Assisted Suicide* (Cambridge: Harvard University Press, 1998) at 120-47 at 144-5. See also R.M. Hare, "Euthanasia: A Christian View" 2 (1) (Summer 1975) Philosophic Exchange.
[37] Indeed, s.2(a) of the *Canadian Charter of Rights and Freedoms*, Part I of the *Constitution Act, 1982*, being Schedule B to the *Canada Act 1982* (UK), 1982, c.11 guarantees that "2. Everyone has the following fundamental freedoms: (a) freedom of conscience and religion; (b) freedom of thought, belief, and expression, including freedom of the press and other media of communication; (c) freedom of peaceful assembly; and (d) freedom of association."
[38] The Seventh, Third and Tenth Commandments, respectively.
[39] For further discussion of the religious sanctity of life arguments, the reader is directed to R. Gillon, "Suicide and Voluntary Euthanasia: Historical Perspective" in A.B. Downing, ed., *Euthanasia and the Right to Death* (Los Angeles: Nash, 1969), and G. Williams, *The Sanctity of Life and the Criminal Law* (New York: Knopf, 1957) Chapter 8.
[40] *Criminal Code*, R.S.C. 1985, c.C-46, s.34.

times of war. Suicide is legal.[41] Therefore, more than a simple recitation of the principle is needed to ground a prohibition of assisted suicide and euthanasia.

Second, if "killing is wrong" is an absolute principle, then suicide and the withdrawal of potentially life-sustaining treatment are wrong. These activities are not and ought not to be illegal in Canada. Unless one is willing to endorse recriminalizing these activities, one cannot logically claim an absolute "killing is wrong" principle as grounds for rejecting assisted suicide and voluntary euthanasia. One can logically claim a limited principle of "killing is wrong" if one can explain why the principle leads to the prohibition of assisted suicide and euthanasia, but not the withdrawal of potentially life-sustaining treatment. However, the distinctions commonly relied on to do so have been considered and rejected earlier in this presentation.

SUFFERING AS A SOURCE OF MEANING

It is frequently argued that suffering has value as a source of meaning and understanding and that assisted suicide and euthanasia, in cutting short suffering, deny the realization of this value.[42] However, not all people find value in suffering. The Judeo-Christian tradition, to which this view of suffering can be traced, should not be imposed upon non-believers. Obviously, those who find value in suffering should be free to suffer. However, those that do not should not be forced to endure suffering in which they do not find value.

Furthermore, to accept the argument from suffering could take us to a prohibition on anaesthesia and other medical interventions aimed at the alleviation of suffering. If it is wrong to cut short suffering and thus deny the realization of the value of suffering, then it is wrong to provide analgesia, anaesthesia and

---

[41] Suicide was illegal in Canada but was removed from the *Criminal Code* in 1972.
[42] See e.g., L. Dionne, Director General, Maison Michel Sarrazin, Quebec, testimony before the Senate Committee on Euthanasia and Assisted Suicide. Senate of Canada, *Proceedings of the Senate Special Committee on Euthanasia and Assisted Suicide*, No. 13 (6 July 1994). See also E.H. Kluge, *The Ethics of Deliberate Death* (New York, 1981) 32-3. The theme of meaning through suffering is illustrated in V. Frankl, *Man's Search For Meaning: An Introduction to Logotherapy* (New York: Simon and Schuster, 1962).

surgical interventions directed at pain relief. These activities are and ought to be permitted in our society. Therefore, the argument from suffering against assisted suicide and euthanasia fails.

Finally, this argument is applied inconsistently across categories. If the value of suffering precludes permitting assisted suicide and euthanasia, then it also precludes withholding and withdrawal of potentially life-sustaining treatment. These latter forms of assisted death also cut short suffering and thus deny the realization of the value. So long as the withholding and withdrawal of treatment are permitted, so too should be assisted suicide and euthanasia.

SLIPPERY SLOPES

The slippery slope argument is commonly expressed in the following terms. If society allows assisted suicide and voluntary euthanasia, then there will be a slide toward the bottom of a slippery slope and many clearly unacceptable practices will become prevalent[43] (we will slide toward allowing involuntary euthanasia and thus the killing of demented patients, mentally disabled humans, indigent humans and any other group deemed to be "unfit" for continued existence).

Now the question of whether people would *in fact* move to involuntary euthanasia if they moved to assisted suicide and voluntary euthanasia is an empirical one.[44] Obviously, we have no direct empirical data on whether people in Canada would in fact over the next five, ten or 20 years move from accepting assisted suicide and voluntary euthanasia to accepting involun-

---

[43] See G. Crelinston, "Mercy Killing: Active Euthanasia Is Not Part of Medicine and It Should Be Rejected" (21 Oct. 1991) *Montreal Gazette* at B3; Special Senate Committee on Euthanasia and Assisted Suicide, *Of Life and Death; Report on the Special Senate Committee on Euthanasia and Assisted Suicide* at 56-7. [*Of Life and Death*].

[44] I am departing from the convention of describing the two types of slippery slopes as logical and psychological (although cited to a number of differing originating sources, I have traced the logical/psychological slippery slope distinction back to J. Rachels in S. Spicker and T. Engelhardt, eds., *Philosophical Medical Ethics: Its Nature and Significance* (Boston: Reidel, 1977) at 65). I have changed the name from "psychological slippery slope" to "empirical slippery slope" because there is not necessarily a psychological component to the empirical slippage and both psychological and non-psychological barriers can be placed on this slope.

tary euthanasia. In the absence of such specific data, many turn to history and to other countries in search of evidence as to whether slippage would *in fact* follow decriminalization. This is where a careful analysis of the historical experience of the Nazis and the contemporary experience of the Netherlands and other countries in which assisted suicide is legal becomes relevant. Unfortunately, I cannot provide you today with the data that support my rejection of the Nazi and Netherlands slippery slope arguments (it takes more than 30 pages to do so).[45] However, I can give you the guts of the refutation of the Netherlands slippery slope argument as it is the most important.

It is frequently stated that the Netherlands moved to a permissive regime with respect to assisted suicide and voluntary euthanasia and then slid down the slope to involuntary euthanasia.[46] It is then argued that if Canada decriminalized assisted suicide and voluntary euthanasia, Canada too would slide to the objectionable bottom of the slippery slope.

However, the Dutch experience does not provide a basis on which to conclude that assisted suicide and euthanasia should not be decriminalized in Canada. Rather, it provides a basis for proceeding carefully and developing a permissive regime that places barriers on the slope and contains mechanisms by which any slippage down the slope can be detected (and, thereafter, rectified).

In my effort to accurately assess the force of the slippery slope argument grounded in the Dutch experience, I will reject a number of the most common and/or egregious misinterpretations and misrepresentations found in the literature. I will then suggest a number of responses that might be made to the Netherlands-based slippery slope argument.

---

[45] *Dying Justice, supra* note 1, at 106-32, "Slippery Slope Arguments".
[46] See, e.g., H. Hendin, "Seduced by Death: Doctors, Patients and the Dutch Cure" (1994) 10 Issues in Law & Medicine 123-68; H. Hendin, *Seduced by Death: Doctors, Patients and the Dutch Cure* (New York: W.W. Norton, 1996); H. Hendin, C. Rutenfrans and Z. Zylicz, "Physician-Assisted Suicide and Euthanasia in the Netherlands: Lessons from the Dutch" (1997) 277 J.A.M.A. 1720-22; R. Fenigsen, "A Case against Dutch Euthanasia" (1989) 19 Hastings Center Report 22-30; C.F. Gomez, *Regulating Death: Euthanasia and the Case of the Netherlands* (New York: Free Press, 1991).

MISINTERPRETATIONS AND MISREPRESENTATIONS

Consider the following statements about the Netherlands found in the literature[47] and in public debate on this issue:

- Euthanasia is widespread
- Euthanasia is available on demand
- Palliative care is absent
- Non-voluntary euthanasia is widespread
- Non-voluntary euthanasia is increasingly accepted
- Involuntary euthanasia is being performed
- Involuntary euthanasia is increasingly accepted
- Abuses are widespread
- Not one of these statements is true.[48]

THE TEMPORAL SLIPPERY SLOPE

A critical step in the slippery slope argument is that legalization caused the slide down the slippery slope; if that is not true, then the Netherlands-based slippery slope argument against decriminalization loses its force. However, there is no evidence that the shift in policy and practice with respect to the state's response to euthanasia and assisted suicide in the Netherlands caused any slide down a slippery slope.

When the first comprehensive data was released from the 1990 study, no slide attributable to change could be demonstrated because there was no prior data with which to compare.[49] When the 1995 data was released it revealed no slide down a slope.[50]

---

[47] Cites for each of these claims are provided in *Dying Justice, supra* note 1 at 111-118.

[48] Rebuttals for each of the claims noted above are provided in *Dying Justice, supra* note 1 at 111-118.

[49] P.J. van der Maas, J.J.M. van Delden, and L. Pijnenborg, "Euthanasia and Other Medical Decisions Concerning the End of Life" (1992) 22(2) Health Policy.

[50] P.J. van der Maas, G van der Wal, I. Haverkate, C.L.M. de Graaff, J.G.C. Kester, A. van der Heide, J.M. Bosma, D.L. Willems and B.D. Onwuteaka-Philipsen, "Euthanasia, Physician-Assisted Suicide, and other Medical Practices Involving the End of Life in the Netherlands, 1990-1995" (1996) 335 N.E.J.M. 1699-1705.

THE COMPARATIVE INTERNATIONAL SLIPPERY SLOPE

The slippery slope argument is also grounded in the assumption that the incidence of non-voluntary euthanasia is higher in the Netherlands (where it is permitted in some circumstances) than in those countries where it is illegal. The truth of this assumption has not been empirically demonstrated and indeed there is now data to suggest that the assumption is false. The data available from, e.g., Australia, positively counter the slippery slope argument—3.5% of deaths were "life-ending acts without explicit request of the patient" in Australia vs. 0.7% in the Netherlands.[51]

THE CURRENT CANADIAN LOCATION ON THE SLOPE

The slippery slope argument often implicitly assumes that we are currently at the very top of a slippery slope and must resist any reform that will put us onto the slope and take us inexorably down to the bottom of the slope. However, this assumption is incorrect for we are already on the slope. Assisted suicide and euthanasia are occurring in Canada. For obvious reasons, it is difficult to gain accurate and complete data on the incidence of assisted suicide and euthanasia; they are illegal acts and health care providers are likely to under-report criminal activity. Nonetheless, what studies there are provide some indication of the incidence. For example, the Manitoba study referred to earlier reported that:

- 72% of physicians surveyed believe euthanasia is performed by some physicians.
- 15% of physicians said they had participated in assisted suicide or euthanasia.[52]

CONCLUSION

Careful reflection on the Dutch experience provides information that can be used in the design of a permissive Canadian regime as we attempt to put in place a regime with the greatest possible safeguards against a descent down the slippery

---

[51] H. Kuhse, P. Singer, P. Baume, M. Clark and M. Rickard, "End-of-Life Decisions in Australian Medical Practice" (1997) 166 Med. J. Australia 191 at 191.
[52] Manitoba, *supra* note 16.

slope. However, it does not provide convincing evidence in support of the claim that if Canada decriminalizes assisted suicide and voluntary euthanasia, Canada *will in fact* slide to the objectionable bottom of a slippery slope.

It is also very, very important to emphasize here that there are now other countries that permit euthanasia and/or assisted suicide and that the data being collected there do not support the empirical slippery slope argument.[53] Indeed, they run absolutely counter to it. After an initial increase when assisted suicide was first legalized in Oregon, the Oregon numbers have remained steady and low over the past five years.[54] Furthermore, many of the concerns about decriminalization (e.g., a disproportionate impact on the vulnerable) have not materialized.

First, many patients who choose to obtain the prescription choose not to use it.[55] Clearly, the fact of initiating access to the assistance does not create a sense of obligation to commit suicide (one potential point of vulnerability). Rather, the prescription seems to serve as a "safety net" that some patients ultimately use and others do not.

Second, the individuals who access assistance are largely not members of the vulnerable groups that opponents are concerned with protecting. The majority of those who chose to seek assistance were insured (100%), in hospice care (92%), male (53%), white (97%) and with at least some college education (62%).[56]

Third, the concerns that motivated the majority of those who sought assistance were not those that opponents are concerned about. The most common reasons for requesting assisted suicide were:

- Fear of decreasing ability to do enjoyable activities (89%)

---

[53] This discussion of the Oregon experience is taken from Jocelyn Downie and Simone Bern, "*Rodriguez Redux*", unpublished manuscript on file with the authors.

[54] All information and statistics mentioned are available on the website for the Government of Oregon, online: http://oregon.gov/DHS/ph/pas/ar-index.shtml. [Oregon].

[55] *Ibid.*

[56] *Ibid.*

- Fear of loss of dignity (89%)
- Fear of losing autonomy (79%)[57]

In sum, as noted by Margaret Battin et al. in 2007, "Rates of assisted dying in Oregon and in the Netherlands showed no evidence of heightened risk for the elderly, women, the uninsured (inapplicable in the Netherlands, where all are insured), people with low educational status, the poor, the physically disabled or chronically ill, minors, people with psychiatric illnesses including depression, or racial or ethnic minorities, compared with background populations.... Those who received physician-assisted dying in the jurisdictions studied appeared to enjoy comparative social, economic, educational, professional and other privileges."[58]

PALLIATIVE CARE
Some people ground their opposition to decriminalization of euthanasia and assisted suicide in two arguments relating to palliative care:

- euthanasia and assisted suicide are not necessary if palliative care is available[59]
- a permissive regime with respect to assisted suicide and euthanasia will make palliative care less available (or make it less likely to be made more available).

However, these arguments are grounded in false premises: First, they assume that people seek assisted suicide or euthanasia because of uncontrolled pain or lack of access to palliative care. However, as noted above, the empirical data on the factors that lead to requests for assisted suicide and euthanasia reveals that uncontrolled pain or lack of access to

---

[57] *Ibid.*

[58] Margaret P. Battin, "Legal Physician-Assisted Dying in Oregon and the Netherlands: Evidence Concerning the Impact on Patients in 'Vulnerable' Groups" (2007) J. Med. Ethics 33, 591-7.

[59] Advocates of this argument include E.D. Pellegrino, "The False Promise and Benefit of Killing" in L.L. Emanuel, ed., *Regulating How We Die: The Ethical, Medical and Legal Issues Surrounding Physician-Assisted Suicide* (Cambridge: Harvard University Press, 1988) at 73 and S. Wolf, "Facing Assisted Suicide and Euthanasia in Children and Adolescents" in Emanuel, at 188.

palliative care is not the only, or even the most common, reason people seek assisted suicide or euthanasia.[60] Access to adequate pain control and palliative care may reduce—but certainly will not eliminate—requests for assisted suicide or euthanasia.

Second, adequate pain control and palliative care are unavailable to many people and will remain so for the foreseeable future. Indeed, the federal government made clear its position recently—it cut the budget for the Palliative Care Secretariat from $1.7 million last year to $470,000 for the upcoming year.[61] This at a time when approximately 15% of Canadians have access to hospice palliative care.[62] This at a time when assisted suicide and euthanasia are illegal.

Third, the experience in the Netherlands and Oregon also disputes the validity of this argument. Indeed, following the introduction of the Oregon legislation, improvements have been made in care of the dying[63] and Oregon has remained a leader in palliative care.[64] The permissive regimes have not undercut palliative care.

Fourth, not all physical pain can be controlled. Even with the best palliative care in the world, some physical pain cannot be controlled.[65] Assisted suicide and euthanasia will not be rendered completely unnecessary by making pain control and palliative care more widely available.

Fifth, the alleviation of physical pain is not necessarily the same as the alleviation of suffering. For example, individuals

---

[60] Oregon, *supra* note 54.
[61] Canadian Hospice Palliative Care Association, online:
<http://www.chpca.net/home.htm>
[62] *Ibid.*
[63] See, for example, Linda Ganzini, Heidi D. Nelson, Melinda A. Lee et al., "Oregon Physicians' Attitudes About and Experiences With End-of-Life Care Since Passage of the Oregon Death With Dignity Act", JAMA 285 (2001): 2363-2369 and E.R. Goy, A. Jackson, T. Harvath et al., "Oregon Hospice Nurses and Social Workers' Assessment of Physician Progress in Palliative Care over the Past 5 Years", Palliative and Supportive Care (2003) 1(3): 215-9.
[64] See, for example, A. Lagorce and M. Herper, "The Best Places to Die", online: www.forbes.com/2004/04/16/cx_al_mh_bestdietab.html.
[65] See testimony before the Special Senate Committee on Euthanasia and Assisted Suicide of Brian Mishara, Elizabeth Latimer and Balfour Mount. *Special Senate Cte.*, No. 2 (20 April 1994) at 26, No. 4 (4 May 1994) at 16, and No. 5 (11 May 1994) at 30, respectively.

whose physical pain is controlled by morphine may suffer from incessant vomiting and other forms of extreme physical discomfort. Individuals may also suffer from mental anguish such as grief and fear. Such non-physical suffering cannot always be controlled by pain control or palliative care. Thus, proper pain control and palliative care will reduce—but not eliminate—the number of requests for euthanasia and assisted suicide.

Sixth, pain control and palliative care are not attractive options for some individuals. Some consider the means of controlling the pain unacceptable. For example, total sedation[66] might be required to control pain, yet some individuals would find total sedation to be worse than death. For some, the religious overtones of palliative care render it unacceptable.[67]

Seventh, the argument could just as easily be applied to the withholding and withdrawal of potentially life-sustaining treatment as to assisted suicide and euthanasia. If adequate pain control and palliative care were made available to all, refusals of treatment would drop. Therefore, until pain control and palliative care are available to all, refusals of treatment should not be respected. However, so long as this argument is not used to restrict respect for refusals of treatment, it cannot be used to restrict access to assisted suicide and euthanasia.

Before leaving this discussion of palliative care, I should emphasize that nothing that I have said goes against vigorous expansion of access to better pain control and symptom management for all Canadians. Indeed, I believe that such expansion is absolutely critical for appropriate care of patients as it increases the options available to patients and thereby contributes to respect for autonomy and dignity. It also reduces suffering. Nonetheless, palliative care and other forms of pain control and symptom management must remain options to be chosen or rejected by patients. The availability or unavailability of these

---

[66] Total sedation is defined by the Senate Committee on Euthanasia and Assisted Death as "the practice of rendering a person totally unconscious through the administration of drugs without potentially shortening that person's life." *Of Life and Death, supra* note 43, at 33.

[67] See, e.g., Arn Shilder, British Columbia Persons with AIDS, testimony before the Special Senate Committee on Euthanasia and Assisted Suicide. *Senate Special Cte.,* No. 16 (28 Sept. 1994).

The Ends of Life and Death:
Public Policy, Spirituality and the Law

options must not be used to deny the selection of other options, such as assisted death.

On the basis of the preceding arguments (and other arguments I did not have time to cover today), I conclude that assisted suicide and euthanasia should have the same legal status as the withholding and withdrawal of potentially life-sustaining treatment. A permissive but regulated regime should be used for not only the withholding and withdrawal of potentially life-sustaining treatment and the provision of potentially life-shortening symptom relief, but also assisted suicide and voluntary euthanasia. Therefore, assisted suicide and euthanasia should not be prohibited where a free and informed request for assisted suicide or euthanasia is made by a competent individual.

In the end, then, while I believe that end-of-life law and policy is inextricably linked up with spirituality, we must not think that this leaves us victim to intractable conflict. Rather, we need to actively seek respectful engagement. And I believe that such respectful engagement will lead most (although certainly not all) Canadians to conclude that the law should be changed and we should decriminalize euthanasia and assisted suicide.

I certainly hope that Canadians will engage and will ultimately demand that legislatures confront these and related questions. If we fail to speak and they fail to act, many Canadians will continue to suffer and we will all continue to fail in our efforts to truly care for the dying. And surely that, and perhaps the *hokey pokey*, is what it's all about.

 3

The End of a Life:
Notes from a Narrow Ridge

Karen Lebacqz, BA, MA, PhD
Robert Gordon Sproul Professor of Theological Ethics, Emerita,
Pacific School of Religion, Berkeley

Many of us slept little the week that ended March and began April of 2005. We sat riveted to our television sets where two deaths unfolded: the first, that of a young woman catapulted into the national spotlight because of a long series of legal battles; the second, that of an old and revered pontiff, ruler of the Roman Catholic Church for more than a quarter of century. The young woman's death was controversial, the pontiff's death not controversial but appropriately sad. Theresa Marie Schiavo and Pope John Paul II became parables of "bad" and "good" dying. Here I focus on the death of Terri Schiavo, but I view that death through a lens informed by the irony in witnessing these two deaths in tandem.

At first glance, it seems as though Terri Schiavo's death should be a jewel of a case study. Dena Davis once argued that good ethics requires 'thick' rather than 'thin' cases.[68] The typical case is 'thin': personal identifiers and particularities are removed to preserve confidentiality. To the extent that ethics is a matter of locating morally relevant features of a case,[69] however, it is precisely particularities that may matter. Thick description should therefore assist ethical analysis. Terri Schiavo's case is 'thick description' at its utmost. Although the early years were largely private, once Terri's husband and her family of origin

---

[68] Dena S. Davis, "Rich Cases: The Ethics of Thick Description," *Hastings Center Report* v.21, no.4 (July/August 1991): 12-18.
[69] I have argued elsewhere that locating morally relevant differences is one of two crucial aspects of ethical reasoning. See Karen Lebacqz, "Bad Science, Good Ethics," *Theology and Science* v.1, no.2, October 2003: 193-201.

became embroiled in legal proceedings, almost every facet of the 15-year dispute became public—perhaps too public![70] There is no dearth of detail here, but a plethora of facts, opinions, claims and counterclaims. The court documents alone would fill a museum.[71] The very thickness of this case makes it a daunting task to sort through the morass and locate morally relevant factors. Trial dates and outcomes are relatively indisputable; almost every other 'fact' is disputed by the parties,[72] though the courts clearly sided with some presentations over others.

It will be my argument that those very disputes are indicative of some deep issues that go beyond a simple effort to determine what happened and what should have been done. Drawing largely on the books recently published by Terri's family of origin and by her husband,[73] I will argue that the disputes suggest that social policy should pay attention to some neglected questions. There are many questions that might merit ethical analysis; I limit my attention to some questions related to the complexities of truth and its implications for social policy. I should also acknowledge at the outset that I began this exploration leaning toward the decision that Terri Schiavo's husband

---

[70] Walter Brueggemann argues for the importance of a conversation that does not adopt dominant political discourse. While his argument is made in the context of the needs of a faith community, I think it is applicable where deep symbolic issues are at stake, as they were in Terri Schiavo's case. The dominant legal language took over and confined possibilities, as I will demonstrate later. See Brueggemann, "The Legitimacy of a Sectarian Hermeneutic: 2 Kings 18-19," in Mary C. Boys, ed. *Education for Citizenship and Discipleship* (New York: Pilgrim Press, 1989).

[71] For a relatively accessible summary, see Matt Conigliaro's *Abstract Appeal* webpage at http://abstractappeal.com/schiavo/infopage.html. It is no wonder that numerous books have been written about this complicated case; condensing it into an essay is no easy task!

[72] For example, it is not disputed that Terri collapsed, but the reasons for the collapse are very much in dispute and might be quite relevant to ethical decision-making. If her husband Michael was responsible for her collapse, as the Schindlers suggest (*A Life*, 123,131), then he should not have been given power of life and death over Terri.

[73] Mary Schindler and Robert Schindler, with Suzanne Schindler Vitadamo and Bobby Schindler, *A Life That Matters: The Legacy of Terri Schiavo – A Lesson for Us All* (New York: Warner Books, 2006), [Hereafter: *A Life*]); Michael Schiavo (with Michael Hirsh), *Terri: The Truth* (New York: Penguin Group, 2006) [Hereafter: *The Truth*]

Michael made—the withdrawing of Terri's feeding tube. I therefore have bent over backwards to balance that bias and give credit to Terri's family of origin, in order to be fair to both parties.

We know this much: at age 26, Terri Schiavo collapsed, was rushed to the hospital, and appeared to have suffered anoxia for a time sufficient to cause some permanent and irreversible brain damage. At the outset, all parties hoped that the damage was *not* irreversible; several experimental protocols as well as routine therapy were attempted. After several years, Terri's husband Michael, who had been appointed her legal guardian, came to believe that Terri's functioning could not be improved.[74] Claiming that Terri would not have wanted to live in a permanent vegetative state,[75] he began legal proceedings to withdraw nutrition and hydration, which were provided by tube. Terri's family of origin—her parents and brother and sister, referred to here collectively as the Schindlers—resisted the withdrawing of the feeding tube. The dispute went through many trials and appeals, and Terri's feeding tube was withdrawn and reinserted several times. Finally, it was withdrawn on March 18, 2005, and she died officially on March 31, 2005.[76]

Beyond these basic facts, however, almost all aspects of this case are contested. Michael Schiavo claims that he was trying to honour Terri's own wishes in seeking to remove her feeding tube. The Schindlers charge that he wanted her dead so that he could inherit her estate and remarry. He counters that he offered to donate all the proceeds from her estate to charity, and that the Schindlers themselves urged him to start a new relationship.[77] The "Schiavo case," as both sides came to call it (albeit with some reluctance), became for some a paradigm of honouring the patient's wishes to die rather than to live per-

---

[74] He claims that he came to this decision after two doctors told him she was PVS. *The Truth*, 87; 145.

[75] *The Truth*, 101, 115, 94.

[76] Believing that she had in fact died on the date of her collapse, Michael Schiavo put the following inscription on her gravestone: "Departed this earth February 25, 1990; At peace March 31, 2005."

[77] *The Truth*, 125, 241; 57.

manently in vegetative state, but became for others a paradigm of greed and murder.[78]

The reliability of claims on all sides is contestable.[79] Having the 'thick' description, then, is marginally helpful for establishing factual truth and more helpful for reading between the lines to find morally relevant features that have been neglected and that suggest deeper dimensions of truth. It is for this reason that I offer the phrase "notes from a narrow ridge." The phrase comes from the book of that title edited by Dena Davis and Laurie Zoloth, who took the image from Martin Buber.[80] Buber uses the narrow ridge to connote that he stands not on a "broad upland" of sure statements about the absolute, but on "a narrow rocky ridge between the gulfs where there is no sureness of expressible knowledge, but [only] the certainty of meeting what remains undisclosed."[81] With regard to the Schiavo case, there is no sureness of expressible knowledge; my focus must be on meeting that which remains undisclosed.

My explorations have inclined me to believe that many, possibly most, of Michael Schiavo's factual claims can be substantiated by evidence provided on both sides. This is consonant with what the courts found repeatedly. However, factual truth leaves me dissatisfied. While courts must address determinations of fact within the framework of the law, there are significant moral issues ill disclosed by fact and law alone. Indeed, it may be the very framework of the law that needs re-examination. Fact is not the same as truth. There is another truth that we ignore at our peril. That truth currently remains undisclosed, and part of my purpose is to disclose it to the best of

---

[78] The Schindlers use the term "murder." *A Life*, 225.

[79] Several Guardians ad Litem (GAL) were appointed for Terri during those years: John H. Pecarek, Richard L. Pearse, Jr. and Jay Wolfson. These court-appointed investigators and advocates presumably are able to step back from personal involvement, and their reports may be more reliable than family reflections. However, objections were raised by the Schindlers to GAL decisions that went against them and by Michael Schiavo to GAL decisions that went against him! Judge Greer also seems to have functioned as a GAL for Terri, and his involvement is strenuously contested by the Schindlers.

[80] Dena S. Davis and Laurie Zoloth, eds., *Notes from a Narrow Ridge: Religion and Bioethics* (Hagerstown, MD: University Publishing Group, 1999).

[81] Quoted as the preface to Davis and Zoloth.

my ability. Hence, I will argue for a different understanding of truth—an understanding that goes beyond fact to incorporate relational truth on both individual and societal levels.

Let us begin with the legal framework. Under Florida law, the legality of withdrawing nutrition and hydration from Terri Schiavo rested on three determinations.[82] First, was she in permanent vegetative state (PVS),[83] such that there was no hope of improvement in her cognition? Second, could she survive without "artificial" nutrition and hydration (i.e., the feeding tube)?[84] Finally, would it have been her desire to die rather than to live in PVS on artificial nutrition and hydration?

Terri's husband Michael contended over the years that the answer to all three of these questions was affirmative: Terri was in PVS,[85] she could not survive without artificial nutrition and hydration[86] and she had indicated clearly that she did not wish to live in such a condition.[87] The courts consistently agreed, finding that Terri was in PVS, that there was 'clear and convincing evidence' of her desire not to be kept alive in that state, and that the removal of the feeding tube[88] would result in her death.

However, Terri's family of origin contested each claim. The Schindlers contended that Terri exhibited voluntary action

---

[82] Florida law established two criteria that had to be met before a feeding tube could be removed: first the patient had to be in PVS, and second, there had to be "clear and convincing evidence" of the patient's wishes regarding removal of nutrition and hydration. Florida State Law 765.101(12) defines PVS as permanent and irreversible condition of unconsciousness in which there is both the absence of voluntary action or cognitive behaviour and an inability to communicate or interact purposefully with the environment. (*The Truth*, 138)

[83] A vegetative state is considered "persistent" after 30 days, "permanent" after 3 months following anoxia or 12 months following trauma. Since Terri's state lasted for many years, if it was indeed vegetative, then she was in permanent vegetative state. But this is precisely what is contested; see the discussion below.

[84] Terminology is difficult. I do not like the term "artificial," but it is common and was used in court proceedings, so I use it here.

[85] *The Truth*, 87, 145, 205, 211.

[86] *The Truth*, 230.

[87] *The Truth*, 145.

[88] Most of the dispute spoke about removing the feeding *tube*. However, the issue is not about the tube itself, but about providing nutrition and hydration. Some commentators argue that the tube should not be removed even when nutrition and hydration are terminated, as medicines can be administered through the tube. See "Declaration of James P. Kelly, M.D." in *A Life*, 248.

such as attempting to speak and that she interacted purposefully with her environment—for example, by following them with her eyes or by laughing appropriately when addressed.[89] They therefore believed that she was not in PVS[90] and that improvement in her cognition was possible, and they enlisted medical experts to support these contentions.

They also contested the claim that Terri could not swallow and therefore that provision of "artificial" nutrition and hydration was necessary.[91] Swallowing tests were performed on Terri a number of times (in 1990, 1991 and 1992) and she was examined by speech pathologists almost yearly through 1997; all of these tests led to the conclusion that, although she could swallow saliva, she could not take food or hydration by mouth and would be at great risk of aspirating food or water if direct administration were attempted.[92] In spite of these test results, her family of origin reports attempting to give her food directly[93] and they continued to believe that, with appropriate rehabilitative therapy, Terri could have been brought to the point where she could survive without a feeding tube. Thus, they contended that Terri had been deprived of needed therapy.

Finally, the Schindlers argued that Terri would not have chosen death over a life with limitations, even severe ones. Drawing on her background as a Roman Catholic, they contended that she would have valued her life even with severe limitations.

The legal focus of the "Schiavo case" was on these various claims about Terri's condition and her wishes. Complications arose at every turn. First, there are questions regarding diagnosis. That Terri had extensive brain damage is admitted

---

[89] *A Life,* 40, 95, 117.

[90] In the hearing held in January 2000, the Schindler's lawyer stipulated that Terri was indeed in PVS. According to Mary Schindler, the family was shocked at this stipulation. Schindler et al., *A Life,* 68. They return over and over to the assertion that Terri was not PVS. See *A Life,* 40, 43, 46, 88, 125, 136, 151, 197, 214f.

[91] One of Terri's care-givers, Heidi Law, claims that she gave Terri ice chips on several occasions and "personally saw her swallow the ice water and never saw her gag." *A Life,* 151.

[92] *The Truth,* 173.

[93] After Terri's feeding tube had been removed, the family of origin brought baby food into Terri's room to attempt to feed her by mouth; however, the nurses obstructed their efforts on grounds that Terri would choke. *A Life,* 103.

even by the Schindlers, who nonetheless hoped for improvement in Terri's condition.[94] Extensive brain damage can be consistent with several diagnoses, of which PVS is only one. Was Terri truly in a persistent vegetative state?[95] During the years of the dispute, Terri was examined by a number of physicians. The majority (and perhaps the most reputable of them[96]) appeared to agree that she was PVS; others disagreed strongly. These others gave hope to the Schindlers, who argued constantly that Terri could be improved with therapy. In 2002, the court asked five physicians to examine Terri, two chosen by her family of origin, two by her husband, and one by the judge. Three videotaped their examinations. At least two saw movement on Terri's part and took this to be evidence of responsiveness beyond PVS state.[97] However, others argued that her movements were merely reflex actions and not indicative of consciousness.[98]

Following Terri's death, an autopsy was performed. The extent of brain damage found in the autopsy led some commentators to believe that the autopsy *confirmed* the diagnosis of PVS. However, as the pathologist himself pointed out, PVS is a clinical diagnosis that must be performed on *living* patients.[99] In a commentary, Joseph Fins and Nicholas Schiff concur, though they do note that the autopsy findings were *consistent with* the definition of PVS of the Multi-Society Task Force report published in 1994.[100]

However, consistency is not the same as proof. Not only must a diagnosis of PVS be made without benefit of autopsy, but

---

[94] "[I]t is incontestably true that Terri was severely brain-injured...." *A Life*, 214.

[95] The more correct term would be 'permanent vegetative state' but the term persistent was used consistently in the debate. Fortunately, PVS can stand for either!

[96] Some medical personnel offered opinions without a personal examination of Terri, leading one physician-bioethicist to declare flatly that "people who think they know what the diagnosis is...or what the morally appropriate response is just because they know the name of the disease or have seen a videotape of the patient are often wrong or foolish or both." Eric Cassell, "The *Schiavo* Case: A Medical Perspective," *Hastings Center Report* 35, no.3 (May-June 2005), 23.

[97] *A Life*, 126f.

[98] This was argued by Dr. Ronald Cranford. See *A Life*, 129.

[99] *A Life*, 215.

[100] Joseph J. Fins and Nicholas D. Schiff, "The Afterlife of Terri Schiavo," *Hastings Center Report* 35, no.4 (July-August 2005), 8.

also, as Fins notes in a separate essay,[101] disorders of consciousness are not as fixed and immutable as was once thought.
Recovery can depend on the patient's age, the site of injury and
the process by which injury occurred (trauma or oxygen
deprivation). The vegetative state may be the first state following
coma, and is generally considered 'persistent' after 30 days and
'permanent' three months following anoxia (or 12 months
following traumatic injury). However, there is a window between
persistent and permanent vegetative state where patients may
enter a "minimally conscious state" (MCS) characterized by
fluctuating awareness of self and environment. The natural
history of MCS is not yet known; reports of patients who wake
up after years in "coma" may in fact be patients who were in
MCS.[102] To the untrained eye, MCS and PVS look very similar;
even neurologists with trained eyes often miss the distinction,
says Fins. Distortions therefore easily enter into interpretation of
symptoms.

　　While the PVS diagnosis was strongly supported by the
courts, Fins' comments about the difficulty in distinguishing PVS
from MCS suggest that it was not altogether unreasonable for
the Schindlers to take Terri's moans, eye movements and smiles
as signs of something other than PVS.[103] Since the difference
between PVS and MCS is difficult to diagnose, and since most
physicians would probably urge that we err on the side of caution, the conclusion that Terri was MCS rather than PVS might
have been warranted.[104] This is the first complicating factor.
Michael Schiavo's contention that Terri was PVS is largely
substantiated, but the Schindlers' hope that she retained more
capacity cannot simply be dismissed as ridiculous, given some of
the complexities of diagnosis. This complicates the determination
of Terri's actual state. Indeed, Michael Schiavo himself at one

[101] Joseph J. Fins, "Rethinking Disorders of Consciousness: New Research and
Its Implications," *Hastings Center Report* 35, no.2 (March-April 2005), 22-24.
[102] The Schindlers, for example, take note of the case of Kate Adamson, whose
feeding tube was removed but subsequently reinserted; she recovered
sufficiently to speak. *A Life*, 231.
[103] They also report that Dr. Ronald Cranford, chosen by Michael Schiavo,
said Terri was responsive to his commands. *A Life*, 124.
[104] Indeed, at least one physician appears to have said this explicitly. See *A Life*,
197.

point declared that Terri was "screaming out in pain."[105] As patients in PVS do not experience pain, this declaration confirms that Terri's symptoms were open to different interpretations.

A second complicating factor affects the determination of Terri's desires. Terri Schiavo was at least nominally Roman Catholic. She had been raised in the faith, she attended Catholic schools and she was married in a Roman Catholic ceremony. Her family of origin considers that fact extremely important. Arguing that Terri was a "practicing, faithful Catholic"[106] and pointing to Roman Catholic values, the Schindlers argue that Terri would have valued her life as having dignity and worth no matter how disabled she had become.[107] Further, they argue that she would never have approved euthanasia, even 'passive' euthanasia by removal of a feeding tube.[108] Her husband, however, contends that Terri was not a practicing Catholic and did not adhere to Catholic views. At the time of her collapse, he argues, she did not belong to a Roman Catholic parish, did not attend mass regularly, never went to confession and hence could not be considered a "practicing Catholic."[109] Indeed, he claims that Terri had said she would countenance abortion in case of disability in the fetus;[110] thus, she did not adhere to crucial and widely known Roman Catholic positions on issues of life and death.[111]

The exact implications of Terri's background and status as Roman Catholic are therefore an additional matter of dispute. What are the implications of that background for her decision-making as an adult? If Terri had not attended mass or gone to confession, she had, indeed, ceased being a "practicing Roman

---

[105] *The Truth*, 105.

[106] *A Life*, 80.

[107] *A Life*, 223.

[108] The withdrawing of life support to enable death to occur is sometimes called "passive" euthanasia and is distinguished from taking action that directly kills the patient, which is then called "active" euthanasia. These terms are contestable, however, as is the presumed ethical distinction between passive and active.

[109] *The Truth*, 126, 163.

[110] *The Truth*, 126.

[111] Michael Schiavo further notes that, in a deposition, Terri's mother, Mary Schindler, herself said that Terri was contemplating divorce; as divorce is against Roman Catholic principles, if true, this claim would suggest that Terri departed from traditional Roman Catholic teachings. See *The Truth*, 91.

Catholic." Michael Schiavo is correct to that extent. However, *faith* is not so simple a matter as *practice*. The aphorism that there are no atheists in foxholes is grounded in the reality that many people who have ceased "practicing" a religion will nonetheless turn to some remembrance of it during times of stress or crisis.[112] Thus, religious values may remain important as determinants of values that underlie decision-making even when one no longer adheres to church rituals. Michael has good evidence for Terri's lapse from practicing Catholicism, but the Schindlers may nonetheless be correct in assuming that she would adhere to some basic Catholic values.

If so, what would those values be and how would they affect a decision about withdrawing nutrition and hydration from someone in PVS? Complicating the faith factor even more is a subtle but important change in Roman Catholic tradition during the time of the Schiavo dispute, and possibly in response to it.[113] Prior to 2004, Roman Catholic moral theologians drew on a long tradition holding that *any* intervention for a patient could be considered "extraordinary" and therefore not mandatory if it presented the patient[114] with too much pain or burden and/or if it offered no hope of recovery.[115] The question at stake was never the *specific technology* or medical procedure, but the patient's own situation. A technology could be 'ordinary' in one case and 'extraordinary' in another, depending on the patient's circum-stances.[116] It was a patient-centred standard. In his 1995

---

[112] Doing hospital chaplaincy, for instance, I have found that people who claim to have no religion nonetheless respond gratefully to a recitation of the 23rd Psalm.

[113] "From 2000 on, people of faith—and not just the Catholic faith—had been sending faxes and emails to Rome trying to get the Vatican involved in Terri's case." *A Life*, 181.

[114] And in most interpretations, the patient's family.

[115] For a review of this history, see Michael R. Panicola, "Catholic Teaching on Prolonging Life: Setting the Record Straight," and Donald E. Henke, "A History of Ordinary and Extraordinary Means," in *Artificial Nutrition and Hydration and the Permanently Unconscious Patient: The Catholic Debate*, eds. Ronald P. Hamel and James J. Walter (Georgetown University Press, 2007).

[116] Repenshek and Slosar suggest that ultimately five criteria emerged for what might be considered extraordinary: (1) the treatment was unattainable; (2) obtaining it would involve great danger or (3) intense pain; (4) it was excessively costly; or (5) it entailed great fear or repugnance. See Mark Repenshek and

encyclical letter *Evangelium Vitae,* for instance, Pope John Paul II had said that, for a determination of what is mandatory, "It needs to be determined whether the means of treatment available are objectively proportionate to the prospects for improvement."[117] If there was no hope of improvement, an intervention was not mandatory. Applied to Terri Schiavo's situation, the provision of nutrition and hydration could have been considered extraordinary treatment and therefore not morally mandatory if there was no hope of improvement or recovery for Terri. This indeed was argued in testimony by Father Gerard Murphy.[118]

However, on March 20, 2004, the very Pope whose own death would so closely follow Terri's[119] offered an opinion that appeared to counter this longstanding tradition.[120] Speaking to participants in an international congress on "Life-Sustaining Treatments and Vegetative State: Scientific Advances and Ethical Dilemmas," the pontiff noted that patients in vegetative state have the right to basic health care, including nutrition and hydration. In particular, "I should like…to underline how the administration of water and food, even when provided by artificial means, always represents a *natural means* of preserving life…" and therefore "should be considered, in principle, *ordinary* and *proportionate,* and as such, morally obligatory…." Finally, the Pope opined that waning hopes for recovery when vegetative state is prolonged for more than a year do *not* ethically justify the cessation of minimal care, including nutrition and hydration.

Some commentators assumed that the net result of the Pope's words was to make clear that nutrition and hydration were morally obligatory in a case such as Terri's.[121] This is what

---

John Paul Slosar, "Medically Assisted Nutrition and Hydration: A Contribution to the Dialogue," *Hastings Center Report* 34, no.6 (2004): 13-16.
[117] Pope John Paul II, *Evangelium Vitae,* no.65.
[118] *A Life,* 80.
[119] The Schindlers note the irony that Pope John Paul II received a feeding tube on the very day that Terri died. *A Life,* 209.
[120] These words were written at a time when the Pope's own health was failing. They were also written at a time when the pontiff was being bombarded with queries and letters regarding Terri Schiavo.
[121] Thomas A. Shannon and James J. Walter, "Implications of the Papal Allocution on Feeding Tubes," *Hastings Center Report* 34, no.4 (2004):18-20. While Shannon and Walter do not discuss Shiavo directly, they do interpret the pope's statement as a striking departure from a long tradition.

her family of origin concluded.[122] However, other commentators suggest that the Pope's statement does *not* mandate nutrition and hydration under all circumstances, emphasizing that the term "in principle" implies possible exceptions, and that the Pope's statement must be taken in a larger context.[123]

If Terri was a believing (if not practicing) Roman Catholic, does her faith tradition mandate acceptance of nutrition and hydration by whatever means are necessary? Roman Catholic commentators will no doubt argue over the precise implications of the Pope's statement for many years. However, Terri collapsed long before the Pope's 2004 statement. In 1990, almost all Roman Catholic theologians concurred in seeing the distinction between "ordinary" and "extraordinary" means as a patient-centred rather than technique-centred distinction. As is clear from Father Murphy's testimony and from the difficulty the Schindlers encountered locating Roman Catholic bishops who would support their position,[124] the preponderance of opinion at the time of Terri's collapse would clearly permit the withdrawing of a feeding tube when there was no hope of recovery. Thus, even if Terri remained strongly Roman Catholic in her basic values, she might well have countenanced the removal of her feeding tube under conditions where she would not recover. The implications of her faith tradition do not point unambiguously in the direction claimed by her family of origin. Supporting this interpretation, of course, are the testimonies from those who claimed that she had, indeed, made clear that she would not want to live in persistent vegetative state.[125]

---

[122] They say, "he didn't mention Terri by name, but in his March 20 address, he made it indisputably clear that we must never deny food and drink to patients in a vegetative state." *A Life*, 182.

[123] Repenshek and Slosar, "Medically Assisted Nutrition and Hydration"; also Lisa Sowle Cahill, *Theological Bioethics: Participation, Justice, Change* (Washington, DC: Georgetown University Press, 2005), 108-110.

[124] The Schindlers sent a letter to every Catholic bishop of every diocese in the United States asking them to speak out in favour of their position and received only three affirmative responses. *A Life*, 82. This suggests that Roman Catholic tradition was indeed compatible with the interpretation that nutrition and hydration might be extraordinary and were not always mandatory.

[125] In addition to Michael Schiavo, both his brother Scott and his sister-in-law Joan gave testimony to this effect. *The Truth*, 158f.

Terri's case is further complicated by the range of players who became involved. Interventions spilled over from medical and legal settings into the political arena, with state and federal legislatures intervening, as well as the Governor of the state of Florida and even the President of the United States.[126] The political involvement was fueled by both left- and right-wing activist groups. Several commentators suggest that the dispute itself took over and the 'righteousness' of groups on both sides made reconciliation of the disputing parties nearly impossible.[127] Several polls showed that most Americans believe the involvement of these political parties was inappropriate.[128] I concur. Indeed, the political posturing and the use of media to garner attention for various advocacy groups reached the level of the disgusting, as Michael Schiavo implies.[129]

Nonetheless, the involvement of pressure groups and politicians points to something important that deserves recognition. There is—and there *should* be—a deep uneasiness in American culture about any action that appears to divest a disabled person of value. Terri was in PVS, but she was not brain dead.[130] She remained a living person, and the limitations on her life did not diminish the value of that life. For instance, Lisa Cahill, who disputes some implications of Pope John Paul II's statement on artificial nutrition and hydration, notes that "the pope's concern about diminishment of respect for those unable to assert their own right to medical resources is well warranted."[131] The law may permit individuals to decide that

---

[126] Schiavo notes that "in a two-day period, *Schiavo* was being dealt with at the Second DCA [District Court of Appeals], the Florida House of Representatives, the Florida Senate, the Florida Supreme Court, the Department of Children and Families, the United States House of Representatives, the United States Senate, and the United States Supreme Court." *The Truth,* 287.

[127] Carl E. Schneider, "Hard Cases and the Politics of Righteousness," *Hastings Center Report* 35, no.3 (May-June 2005): 24-27; Jay Wolfson, "Erring on the Side of Theresa Schiavo: Reflections of the Special Guardian ad Litem," *Hastings Center Report* 35, no.3 (May-June 2005): 16-19.

[128] *The Truth,* 301.

[129] *The Truth,* 171, 326.

[130] The examination report of neurologist Jeffrey Karp noted: "She does not meet the criteria of being brain dead, but...is in a persistent vegetative state." *The Truth,* 123.

[131] Cahill, *Theological Bioethics,* 109.

they would not wish to live under certain conditions, but that legal determination must be carefully circumscribed. When an individual is incompetent, others of necessity must make the decision. This always raises the danger that they will decide based not on the patient's own preferences, but on the discomfort or burden to care-givers or on their inheritance in case of death.

It is no mistake that many of the activist groups who intervened were disability activists. To the extent that Terri became a symbol of life with serious disabilities, their advocacy for Terri holds deep symbolic value.[132] It is consonant with Christian faith that those who are weak and vulnerable are considered deserving of special protection. Thus, while involvement of legislatures may have been inappropriate, the very political turmoil points to an important value that has implications for social policy. In setting social policy, a balance must somehow be struck between protection of individual choices and protection of the value of all life. Legally, it may be simply a matter of determining who has the right to decide for an incompetent patient, but morally, the matter is never that simple.

A final complicating factor in the *Schiavo* case is money. A lawsuit brought by Michael Schiavo against Terri's obstetrician and her primary care physician charged that they failed to diagnose Terri's bulimia; hence, they failed to offer appropriate treatment that might have prevented her collapse. Michael received a settlement in the amount of roughly $1,000,000 U.S. ($750,000 for Terri's care and $300,000 for his loss of spouse).[133] Much of the subsequent acrimony between parties centres on money and its disposition.[134] "From being the closest of allies... we became sudden enemies...";[135] the "Schindler v. Schiavo

---

[132] The third GAL, Jay Wolfson, noted that Terri had indeed become a symbol, though he does not specify of what. See *The Truth*, 250. The Schindlers increasingly began to describe Terri in terms of a life with disabilities—see *A Life* 189, 191, 208.

[133] *The Truth* 58, 74, 77. Because the court found that Terri was 70% responsible for her bulimic condition, the actual settlement represents only 30% of the total consideration.

[134] The Schindlers claim that Michael promised to share the funds with them and reneged on that promise; he claims that he never made such a promise. See Schindler et.al., *A Life*, 52f; Schiavo, *The Truth* [GET]

[135] *A Life*, 49.

battle" followed the settlement.[136] Both parties in dispute accused the other party of wanting access to the money. Both agree that the turning point was on Valentine's Day, 1993, when Michael Schiavo and Robert Schindler had a confrontation about money outside Terri's room.[137]

Each party remembers that crucial confrontation differently. What was actually said will probably never be known. What is clear to any observer, however, is that each reports only part of the story. The Schindlers claim that Michael never told them where the money went; Michael claims that the money for Terri's care was not under his disposition and he did not always know where it went.[138] Michael claims that he was not after the money and had offered to donate any remaining funds to charity upon the removal of Terri's feeding tube;[139] this offer is not mentioned by the Schindlers. Each party accuses the other of not responding to overtures toward reconciliation.[140] That money was the turning point is clear.[141] But equally clear, in my view, is that the disputes cannot simply be reduced to money.[142]

Throughout the long legal battles, both parties believed—and still believe—that they had truth on their side. *"The evidence, the facts, and the truth were on our side,"*[143] asserts Michael Schiavo. *"[E]verything we said was true and everything they said was dishonest,"*[144] claim the Schindlers. At stake here is a fundamental issue about truth: what it is, and what it implies for social policy. The courts sided with Michael Schiavo repeatedly,

---

[136] *The Truth*, 82

[137] *A Life*, 53f.

[138] *The Truth*, 75, 78, 80.

[139] *The Truth*, 122, 125.

[140] *A Life*, 186f; *The Truth*, 109.

[141] This was noted by Judge Greer, who declared that "money overshadows this entire case." See the court decision reproduced in Schiavo, *The Truth*, Appendix 1, p.335.

[142] In her stunning study of cross-cultural conflict, Anne Fadiman suggests that "If you stand at the point of tangency, you can see both sides better than if you were in the middle of either one." (Anne Fadiman, *The Spirit Catches You and You Fall Down*, New York: Farrar, Straus and Giroux, 1997, viii.) If my narrow ridge is at the point of tangency between disputing parties, then perhaps I can see some things that each party ignored.

[143] Schiavo, *The Truth*, 290.

[144] Schindler et al., *A Life*, 83.

and there is good reason to believe that the evidence and facts support his position at most points. However, as noted above, even where the evidence and facts appear to support one side more than the other, there are deeper issues and reasons to believe that an additional 'truth' is being expressed by the other side. Perhaps the most difficult question is whether that deeper truth can be embodied in social policy and law. So I turn now to some reflections on truth.

"Do you swear to tell the truth, the whole truth, and nothing but the truth?" This oath of legal testimony was drummed into my mind at an early age. The oath, and the legal process to which it points, focus on facts and evidence. Anyone who has witnessed a court proceeding knows that rarely if ever do parties tell the 'whole truth.' They answer specific questions and those questions are carefully crafted to avoid certain topics and to delimit answers.[145] Even multiple legal proceedings such as occurred in the Schiavo case are unlikely to uncover the 'whole' truth.[146]

It might seem, then, that personal testimony is a better avenue to truth. Michael Schiavo entitles his book *Terri: The Truth*. At the outset, he states that the "truth" he tries to convey in the book is the truth of his own experiences and feelings throughout the ordeal. Similarly, *A Life That Matters: The Legacy of Terri Schiavo – A Lesson for Us All* is the record of the Schindler's understanding of their long ordeal, and documents their hurts and angers.[147] As simple testimony to feelings, either book might be taken as truthful.

Of course, neither book is confined to feelings; both contain attacks on the other side and claims to veracity regarding facts. Both sides offer their testimonies not simply to express feelings but at least in part to set the record straight regarding factual truth. "The facts have been twisted," declares Michael

---

[145] Michael Schiavo notes, for example, that litigators rarely ask questions to which they do not already know the answers. *The Truth*, 142.

[146] Schiavo admits his naïveté in assuming that testimony to "tell the whole truth" would indeed result in truthful and full statements. *The Truth*, 272. The Schindlers claim that officials in the legal system "made uncovering the truth impossible." *A Life*, 138.

[147] Mary Schindler writes, "even as I write this, twelve years later, I can feel our anger, relive the depths of our pain." *A Life*, 53.

Schiavo—twisted by the Schindlers, by politicians and even by medical practitioners.[148] Similarly, while the Schindlers' book is largely an impassioned plea for a perspective, it nonetheless presents facts to discredit Michael Schiavo.[149] Both testimonies are self-serving. Each ignores evidence or claims presented by the other; when evidence is not ignored, it is dismissed as unreliable.[150] Only the facts that fit their interpretations are given weight. Because all parties in this protracted battle lost someone they loved, and because loss and grief distort judgment, I am inclined to give them all the benefit of the doubt. Each party, I will presume, is telling the truth as they see it. What are we to make of this?

The kindest interpretation here might be that of Judge Greer: "[P]erceptions may become reality to the person having them."[151] Neither party lies deliberately; rather, they merely present their perceptions as reality because perceptions have become reality to them. However, this raises the question of self-deception: are they self-deceived in their perceptions? In a justly famous essay, Stanley Hauerwas and David Burrell argue that humans have an inveterate tendency to self-deception and that if we do not consciously develop practices to counter that tendency, "the condition of self-deception becomes the rule rather than the exception in our lives."[152] Defining self-deception in

---

[148] Schiavo, xiii.

[149] For instance, they go to great lengths to suggest that Michael Schiavo was abusive and known for his temper and that a former girlfriend testified to this. They do not correct this impression by noting the corrections in her testimony under cross examination. *A Life*, 105f.

[150] For example, the Schindlers consistently claim that Terri was "starved to death" (*A Life*, 167) and that she suffered greatly from this process, even though medical opinion asserts that death following removal of nutrition and hydration results from an electrolyte imbalance subsequent to dehydration and that patients do not suffer.

[151] George W. Greer, Circuit Judge, "In Re: the Guardianship of Theresa Marie Schiavo, Incapacitated," Circuit Court for Pinellas County, Florida, Probate Division, File #90-2908GD-003, reproduced in *The Truth*, 334-343 at 339.

[152] Stanley Hauerwas and David B. Burrell, "Self-Deception and Autobiography: Reflections on Speer's *Inside the Third Reich*," in Stanley Hauerwas, *Truthfulness and Tragedy: Further Investigations into Christian Ethics* (Notre Dame: U. Notre Dame, 1977), 82-98.

terms of failure to spell out what we are doing,[153] Hauerwas and Burrell note that our lives are, of necessity, "replete with illusions." Illusions help us cope: "we systematically delude ourselves in order to maintain the story that has hitherto assured our identity."[154] We try to preserve the identity we have created by failing to spell out some of our engagements and their meanings.[155] Ironically, the greater the person's integrity, the greater is the temptation to self-deception, as people with integrity need to see all their actions and meanings as having coherence.

In the case at hand, Terri's parents may have deceived themselves into believing that she was genuinely responsive to them in order to preserve their identity as parents of a child with potential and in order to preserve the 'justness' of their cause. Similarly, Michael Schiavo may have deceived himself into believing that all his actions were simply those of a loving husband and not at all self-serving, even after he began a new relationship and fathered several children by his new partner. Indeed, Michael Schiavo notes that, at the beginning, he told people that Terri recognized his voice. He calls these actions on his own and on the Schindlers' parts "wishful lies."[156] They are not deliberate lies, but rather internal attempts to make reality conform to desire. So strong was their desire that the Schindlers went to great lengths to find physicians who would support their claims that Terri was able to follow them with her eyes, and they dismissed out of hand any evidence to the contrary. While it is tempting to say that they ignored or distorted the truth, it may be more accurate to say that they were themselves deceived about their own actions and purposes.

But there is more to it than this. Joan Scott notes that we tend to assume that knowledge is gained through vision and that vision is direct apprehension of a world that is transparent to

---

[153] I would add: and why we do it.

[154] Hauerwas and Burrell, "Self-Deception," 87.

[155] Take the case of loving parents who contemplate abortion because of genetic defect in the fetus, for instance. In order to preserve their identity as loving rather than selfish parents, they may deceive themselves into thinking that their child to be will suffer and that abortion is to relieve the child's suffering rather than to relieve their own. See Karen Lebacqz, "Abortion: Getting the Ethics Straight," *Logos*, v.3 (1982): 47-60.

[156] *The Truth*, 180.

us.[157] Experience is therefore taken as incontestable evidence of reality. Just so did Terri's family of origin *see* her eyes move and conclude that they were seeing direct evidence of her cognitive abilities. They therefore expected the doctors to "see" the same thing.[158] Most doctors examining Terri, however, also saw her eyes move but interpreted that movement very differently. Direct experience is always interpreted through a lens framed by training and circumstance. Hence, experience is not the direct 'evidence' that we might like it to be. To Mary Schindler, direct experience alone spoke volumes; to the court and medical systems, direct experience is always interpreted through a lens of professional knowledge and training.[159]

The gap between direct experience and the interpretation of it, and the tendency toward self-deception both suggest that truth does not simply emerge from the direct expression of a person's experience.[160] Truthful testimony needs to account for the ways in which experience itself is socially constructed.

---

[157] Joan W. Scott, "The Evidence of Experience," in *The Lesbian and Gay Studies Reader,* Henry Abelove, Michele Aina Barale and David M. Halperin, eds. (New York: Routledge, 1993), 397-415.

[158] "The doctors' examination, whether they were our doctors, Michael's, or the court's, would surely see what I saw: A girl responding. A girl aware." *A Life,* 117.

[159] Mary Schindler also struggled with the fact that the legal system seemed to take over, making decisions that she thought were hers to make, and determining the 'meaning' of Terri's movements and capacities. *A Life,* 60, 173.

[160] Hauerwas and Burrell suggest that a truthful testimony will allow us to 'step back' from our deceptions. An autobiographer, they note, cannot simply recount the events of his or her life. There is no way to avoid writing from the dominant perspective and image of his [or her] time. The key is to show the limits of past perspectives and to see how the current perspective is shaped. For Hauerwas and Burrell, this depends on having a 'master story' that helps to unmask previous deceptions. The story must enable us to acknowledge the evil we perpetrate. Using the case of Albert Speer, the architect who designed Hitler's gas chambers, they note that Speer wanted to avoid any responsibility for the evils of Hitler's regime. He thought he could avoid political involvement by simply doing his job and declaring: "political events did not concern me." Hauerwas and Burrell, "Self-Deception," 91. Ironically and importantly, Mary Schindler also wants to separate herself and her family from the political turmoil surrounding Terri's life and death: "As I said at the beginning, we were not political people—and we are not now." *A Life,* 154. In both cases, the moral agents attempt to hide behind a façade of innocence, disclaiming connection between their personal lives and the political climate surrounding them. Failure

The End of a Life:
Notes from a Narrow Ridge

Hence, while the discrepancies and counter claims in the two personal testimonies do little to establish factual truth, I believe that the value of testimony lies elsewhere. It points us beyond factual truth to *relational* truth. *"When somebody you love dies, you don't get over it,"* claims Terri's mother.[161] Testimony attempts to express something deeper than mere facts; it urges a truth that is *relational*. Truth is not the same as factuality.[162] When a doctor suggested that Terri's movements were only reflexes and were not direct responses to her mother's presence, Mary Schindler says, "I felt that he had dishonoured my bond with my daughter. How *dare* he claim that Terri's look of love, which she never gave to anyone else, was reflex? ...He had taken something pure and covered it with mud."[163] The 'facts' felt like a slap in the face to Mary Schindler. They dishonoured her sense of relationship.

It is the question of relational truth and its implications for social policy that will occupy the remainder of this essay. In admittedly too brief form, I develop an understanding of relational truth drawing on insights from theological, anthropological and medical sources, and then hint at the implications of such an understanding for law and social policy.

I begin with the theological. Theologian Dietrich Bonhoeffer distinguishes factual truth and the deeper truth of relationship.[164] Telling the truth, suggests Bonhoeffer, is "a matter of correct appreciation of real situations and of serious reflection upon them."[165] Because truthful speech addresses a *person* as well as a factual situation, correct appreciation of the

---

to accept responsibility for the connections between the personal and the political is itself a form of self-deception. South African theologian Allan Aubrey Boesak also notes that Westerners tend to want to be 'innocent' of political and power issues, but that it is time to say "farewell to innocence." Allan Aubrey Boesak, *Farewell to Innocence: A Socio-Ethical Study on Black Theology and Power* (Maryknoll, NY: Orbis Books, 1977), 3.

[161] *A Life*, 224. Emphasis added.

[162] For a more extended discussion, see Karen Lebacqz, "A Tale of Truth: Story Theology and Ethical Analysis," in *Doing Theology with Asian Resources: Ten Years in the Formation of Living Theology in Asia*, ed. John C. England and Archie C.C. Lee (Auckland, NZ: Pace Publishing, 1993), pp. 83-100.

[163] *A Life*, 129.

[164] Dietrich Bonhoeffer, *Ethics*, ed. Eberhard Bethge (New York: MacMillan, 1955).

[165] Bonhoeffer, 364.

situation and, hence, truthful utterance "must in each case be different according to whom I am addressing, who is questioning me, and what I am speaking about."[166] Truth is relational. The cynic claims to speak the truth but makes no allowance for human weakness; in speaking blunt "truth" (i.e. facts), the cynic destroys the living truth between people. This is precisely what Mary Schindler reflects when she says that the doctor's words dishonoured her bond with her daughter.

Still, the need to speak a different truth in each situation does not mean that we are free to distort facts or decide what portion of truth we tell to each person. Words have *environments*, suggests Bonhoeffer. Genuine words respect the environment. Suppose a teacher asks a child in front of the class whether it is true that the child's father comes home drunk every night. It is factually true, but the child denies it. For Bonhoeffer, the father's drunkenness is a family secret that is not rightly exposed in the environment of the classroom. Hence, the child's answer, while a lie, "contains more truth... [and] is more in accordance with reality than would have been the case if the child betrayed his father's weakness in front of the class."[167] Bonhoeffer's example may be problematic today, as we are keenly aware of the damage done to children by keeping family secrets such as alcoholism or sexual abuse. However, Bonhoeffer's basic point that truth has *two* points of reference—factual situations *and* human relationships—remains valid. It is possible to speak factual truth and yet fail to be truthful, since truth is not simply about factuality but also about relationship.

Relational truth means that each party in the Schiavo dispute is trying not simply to state facts but to express something 'true' about their relationship with Terri. The diatribes are certainly troubling. One casualty in this prolonged legal battle was civility. Tempers flared, power was used sometimes ruthlessly, outsiders who knew little or nothing about the circumstances stepped in as though they were authorities, the press ran amuck

Bonhoeffer, 365. In *The Joy Luck Club* (New York: GP Putnam's Sons, 1989, p.188), Amy Tan has one of her characters declare: "To each person I told a different story. Yet each version was true...." This aligns with Bonhoeffer's point.
[167] Bonhoeffer, 368.

with charges that were not only untrue but also inflammatory. It is embarrassing to read some of the charges and diatribes by the Schindlers and Schiavo. Yet the very passion with which they speak suggests that something very basic is at stake—the preservation of their sense of relationship with Terri.

Terri's mother wanted desperately for her daughter not to die.[168] Indeed, Mary Schindler wanted to take her daughter home and care for her in spite of her lack of function.[169] While I believe that Terri Schiavo was in PVS and would not have been brought to greater functioning under her mother's care, I nonetheless believe that there is a relational truth here that should be recognized. I illustrate with an example that is not well known in the bioethics arena, but has been famously popular elsewhere.[170]

It is the story of Lia Lee, a beautiful little Hmong child born in California to refugee parents who spoke no English. Lia had epilepsy. When she had seizures, her anxious parents would grab her in their arms and race to the hospital. By the time they arrived, her seizures had typically stopped. Because they spoke no English and there was no translator available, hospital personnel saw only an exhausted looking child. Lia was misdiagnosed for months. Her parents were given medicines that were not for epilepsy and did nothing to contain the seizures. Finally, when Lia went into a 'grand mal' seizure in the hospital, a correct diagnosis was made and proper medications were ordered. However, by this time Lia's parents no longer trusted American medicine, which did not cohere with their cultural paradigms of illness and which had previously failed to control their daughter's seizures. They therefore gave the medications erratically if at all. At one time, they were declared unfit parents and Lia was removed from their care; eventually she was returned to them. But in spite of all efforts, Lia deteriorated. It is

---

[168] Michael Schiavo charges that Terri's mother did not visit Terri regularly; however, he may ignore the demands on Mary Schindler's life, as her husband did indeed sometimes need her care as well.

[169] Michael Schiavo claims that there were financial motives mixed into this desire. I do not deny this, yet I believe that there was also genuine love and desire to be with her child.

[170] Anne Fadiman, *The Spirit Catches You and You Fall Down: A Hmong Child, Her American Doctors, and the Collision of Two Cultures* (New York: Farrar, Strauss and Giroux, 1997).

a long and sad story, ending with a little girl who was declared PVS.[171] She had no gag reflex, no corneal reflexes, no response to deeply painful stimulation and her EEG showed "very flat" brain waves.[172] She continued to breathe, swallow, sleep and wake, snore, grunt and cry.[173]

Although Lia's story comes from a different family and a different culture, its similarities to the story of Terri Schiavo are instructive. Lia's medical condition bears striking resemblance to Terri's—even to the point of Lia making noises and appearing uncomfortable at times.[174] Both Lia and Terri entered PVS as a result of anoxia. Both sets of parents refused to give up on their child. Statements made by Lia's mother and father echo feelings expressed by Terri's parents. Lia's parents insisted on being at her bedside. When the intravenous lines were disconnected from Lia with the expectation that she would then die, her mother says, "At that moment I was so scared it seemed like something was just going up and down my body and I thought I was going to die too."[175] Like Terri, Lia responded to different care-givers: when her mother picked her up, she stopped crying. As with physicians who examined Terri, one of Lia's doctors declared this responsiveness to be "all reflex." It is possible, he suggested, for a person to have "no thoughts, no memories, no conscious life, and yet respond to her mother's touch."[176] Yet, for the parents, the response was meaningful: "When we hold her, she knows it and is smiling," said Lia's father.[177] The lack of capacity of both daughters did not diminish their value in the parent's eyes. Both sets of parents wanted to take their child home to care for her. Lia was in fact sent home with every expectation that she would die. But she did not. Some 20 years later, Lia continues to

---

[171] Anne Fadiman, *The Spirit Catches You and You Fall Down*, 173; 210.
[172] Fadiman, *The Spirit*, 150.
[173] Fadiman, 211.
[174] Fadiman, 172.
[175] Fadiman, 151.
[176] Fadiman, 211.
[177] Fadiman, 211. Lia's father died several years ago. (Personal communication with Fadiman, Spring 2006.)

live at home, totally unresponsive but cared for by an exhausted yet loving mother.[178]

Because Lia was still a small child when she entered PVS, there was no question about honouring her autonomy. This, of course, makes the case strikingly different from Terri Schiavo's in at least one sense. Yet, to loving parents, the age of the child may not be what matters: Terri's parents spoke of her as "a girl" long after she had passed the age of 30, and her mother consistently appealed to care-givers to recognize her feelings because she was a mother.[179] The truth of each story must somehow incorporate this level of parental love. There is a personal relationship that donates its own 'truth' into the situation.[180] In Lia's case, the parents were automatically the decision-makers. Terri's case is more complicated because she was a young adult when she collapsed and she had a husband as well as devoted parents. Legally, her husband became her surrogate decision-maker. Yet I would argue that shutting out the parents does not serve truth well, as it denies a relational truth in the parental bond.

The Second District Court of Appeals gave lip service to that bond, saying "[W]e understand why a parent who had raised and nurtured a child from conception would hold out hope...." However, the Court noted that it was constrained by the law:

---

[178] That the routine of caring for Lia is exhausting cannot be denied. While Lia was a favourite child and her mother still adores her, at times she breaks down and cries and at one point she said, "I am so busy with Lia that I don't know anything else except being alive." Fadiman, 218.

[179] *A Life*, 117.

[180] If we take relational truth seriously in Terri Schiavo's case, some important implications follow. First, it means that we cannot simply turn Terri's situation into a case! Michael Schiavo capitulates to public discourse and uses the term "the Schiavo case" himself. Yet it is clear that Terri is not simply a "case" to either her family of origin or to her husband. For those of us on the outside, it is tempting to see Terri's life and death as a 'case'—a paradigm case to be added to the 'cases' of Cruzan, Quinlan and other well-known bioethics cases. But Terri Schiavo was a living person—a daughter, a sister, a wife, a colleague. These relationships are part of who she was and is; any truth about Terri cannot simply reduce her to a case. Here, Dena Davis' caution about thick and thin description is very apt. Thick description is meant to retain the fullness of human life, not simply to provide more grist for the mill in examining a case.

"The judges on this panel are called upon to make a collective, objective decision concerning a question of law.... [I]n the end, this case is not about the aspirations that loving parents have for their children. It is about Theresa Schiavo's right to make her own decision, independent of her parents and independent of her husband."[181]

In other words, the law very precisely made it impossible to recognize relational truth. Florida law mandated that the decision about Terri's life rest solely on the determination of what her own wishes would have been, "independent" of both her family of origin and her marriage.

It is for this reason that I argue that the framework of the law itself may be faulty. Current bioethics law is very "autonomy" oriented, at least in the United States. Increasingly, commentators are pointing to the deficiencies of autonomy as the basis of social policy. In "What I Learned from *Schiavo*," lawyer Gerald Witherspoon notes that "good lives and deaths are those deeply intertwined with, and deeply respectful of, the lives and deaths of others."[182] He suggests wording for advance directives based on recognition of this relational truth. Religious commentators are solidly in agreement. For example, Cahill argues that "insofar as autonomy is the main impetus behind the movement for physician-assisted suicide ... this movement should be and is resisted by most religious communities...."[183] Values such as community, covenant, solidarity, reciprocity and altruism suggest that autonomy is too narrow a base for law in the medical arena.

Of course, incorporating relational truth into law would be no easy task. While I have argued above that the claims of parents should have more weight than they did in the Schiavo case, Michael's claims would also have to carry weight. At the beginning, Michael and Terri's parents desired the same thing for Terri. But over time, their desires—and their sense of relational truth—diverged. Michael Schiavo claims that in his fight to end Terri's life, he was honouring his relationship with Terri by keeping a promise to her: her gravestone is inscribed "I

181 *The Truth*, 227f.
182 Gerald S. Witherspoon, "What I Learned from *Schiavo*," *Hastings Center Report* 37, no.6 (2007): 17-20.
183 Cahill, *Theological Bioethics*, 91.

kept my promise."[184] Thus, his own understanding of relational truth might still have pushed in the opposite direction from the Schindlers. Promises are serious. It takes a great deal to override them, and it should do so. The love of Terri's parents alone might not be enough to tip the balance away from Michael's promise. Is there anything that might help us tip the balance in one direction or another?

Here my thoughts are only suggestive, and I stand on a narrow ridge indeed. Relational truth has social as well as personal dimensions. A second story—the story of Cardinal Jackson, told by physician David Schiedermayer—illustrates this truth.[185] At the time of narration, Cardinal Jackson is a 79-year old woman, cared for at home by her daughter. Schiedermayer has been treating her for six years. He describes Cardinal as "lights are on, but nobody's home."[186] Like Terri and Lia, Cardinal is "mindless" and has been for ten years. Like Terri, she has a feeding tube.

Schiedermayer's medical students ask him why he continues to visit the family and provide medical care for Cardinal. Why not let her die, they ask? He answers: "I asked the daughter five times to stop tube feeding … and she said definitely no each time. That's why not." He also says, "Six years of knowing her…. That's why not." He adds: "I am obsessed with her eyes. They are green as a Georgia hill, humid, warm and smoky…. I can't stand to think of the fire dying in those green eyes."

From the fact that Schiedermayer has asked the daughter to consider removing Cardinal's feeding tube, we can conclude that he would not judge it wrong to do so. "I know how to stop treatment and let dying happen," he says. Whether it is the *right* thing to do, however, depends on many factors. Most of those factors are relational. Some derive from the daughter's relationship with her mother: her willingness to care for her mother warrants continued life support. Some derive from the

---

[184] A picture of Terri's gravestone can be found in *The Truth* just before p. 173.

[185] David Schiedermayer, "House Calls to Cardinal Jackson," *Second Opinion*, v. 17, n.4: 34-41; April 1992.

[186] In an interesting parallel, Lia's doctors also claimed that she was "no one's home, the lights are out." Fadiman calls this "gallows-humor slang." Fadiman, 173.

doctor's own relationship to Cardinal: the length of his relationship, his sense of her dignity, and his fascination with her eyes. Schiedermayer permits both his own relationship and the daughter's relationship with Cardinal to override the futility of continued feeding. Just so might personal relationships with Terri override the futility of continuing artificial nutrition and hydration.

But there is more. In addition to the daughter's relationship and his own relationship with Cardinal Jackson, Schiedermayer gives us a hint of something else. When listing the reasons why he continues to make house calls and treat Cardinal, Schiedermayer adds: "A socioeconomic history of discrimination and mistreatment. A tradition of poor health care and nontreatment. The need to show her somehow we're not abandoning her. That's why not." There is a hint here that social history and social relationships matter also: where there has been discrimination and one has been neglected, it becomes incumbent to maintain and support relationship and care. Relational truth is not simply individual, but social: debts are owed to those who have experienced discrimination and neglect.

Terri's situation does not bear exact parallels to these social dimensions. There is no hint here that Terri has suffered a history of discrimination and mistreatment. Nonetheless, it may be important to consider whether there are relational factors on a social level that should be considered. While Terri's health care was not "poor" in general, her primary physician and treating gynaecologist were held partly responsible for her collapse because they had failed to observe possible signs of anorexia and its implications. But social responsibility should go beyond these parties as well. If Terri's collapse was indeed due to anorexia or bulimia,[187] then social pressures to be thin might have influenced Terri's condition. Some of these pressures may have come from within her family,[188] but beyond her family of origin lurks a society that may have to bear some responsibility for Terri's obsession with being thin. In *The Beauty Myth*, written around the

---

[187] This has been widely supposed but in fact was never conclusively determined. See the autopsy report excerpts, *The Truth*, 347.
[188] Very troubling here is Michael Schiavo's charge that Terri's own father ridiculed her for being overweight; see *The Truth*, 12.

time of Terri's collapse, Naomi Wolf noted that 95% of bulimics in the United States are women, and that more young women were dying of anorexia each year than the total number of deaths from AIDS as of that date.[189] If Terri's collapse reflects social pressures on young women, then societal responsibility may include providing care beyond what seems immediately 'reasonable' in terms of Terri's projected outcome.

Further, once this case became public and Terri's life took on symbolic meaning for disabled people, Terri's life in one sense was no longer simply her own. She represented something larger than herself. Disability rights activists argued for Terri's continued life as a symbol that people with disabilities are not simply abandoned or pushed aside. Their advocacy does not automatically mean that Terri should have been kept alive, but it does echo Schiedermayer's concern that discrimination and history matter to current decisions and that those who are diminished in capacity should not be abandoned. Terri's death took on a larger meaning than simply the life of one person. The political dimensions cannot simply be ignored. As troubling as the specific interventions of advocacy groups might be, those groups make an important point when they advocate for the worth of life with disabilities.

The Courts were forced by law to uphold Terri's autonomy. In so doing, at least one court acknowledged specifically that it put relationships aside. If truth is relational, however, then social policy and law are woefully inadequate when they recognize only autonomous decision-making rather than relationships. If we take relational truth seriously, autonomy alone should not always trump others' desires, especially when life and relationship are at stake. Bobby Schindler expresses this well when he declares, "there is no right to *absolute* personal autonomy. We have obligations to each other and to God."[190]

---

[189] Naomi Wolf, "Hunger," excerpted in Karen Lebacqz, ed., *Sexuality: A Reader,* (New York: Pilgrim Press, 1999), p.286. See also Susan Bordo, *Unbearable Weight: Feminism, Western Culture and the Body* (Berkeley: University of California Press, 1993). For a more contemporary perspective on this problem, see Courtney E. Martin, *Perfect Girls, Starving Daughters: The Frightening New Normalcy of Hating Your Body* (Free Press, 2007).
[190] *A Life,* 221f.

Whether law and social policy can find a way to honour relational truth is perhaps questionable. There are hints in this direction, however, in the work being done in other arenas. "Restorative justice" programs are springing up around the world to replace or supplement criminal justice systems. Such programs recognize that reality is relational and that crime destroys relationship; the purpose of restorative justice programs is to restore relationships as far as possible. In the arena of bioethics and social policy, we have seen the ascendancy of autonomy to the point where relationships are ignored. The prioritizing of autonomy in bioethics has become problematic. From my vantage point on a narrow, rocky ridge, I believe that it is time for policy in bioethics, which so long has tipped the scales in favour of autonomy, to attempt to incorporate relationships and relational truth.

4

Dying with Dignity:
A Contemporary Challenge
in End-of-Life Care

Harvey M. Chochinov, MD, PhD
Director, Manitoba Palliative Care Research Unit, CancerCare Manitoba
Genevieve Thompson, RN, PhD, CHPCN(C)
Post-doctoral fellow, Manitoba Palliative Care Research Unit

Dignity is a common term used in everyday discourse. Yet despite this familiar use it lacks conceptual specificity when applied in clinical practice. For those involved in health care, preserving the dignity of patients is a major concern, and implies a course of action to be taken (Anderberg et al., 2007; Haddock, 1996). Some would argue that preserving patient dignity is one of the most important ethical considerations when providing care to a patient (Anderberg et al., 2007; Jacelon et al., 2004). Attending to concerns of preserving and augmenting dignity requires special consideration when an individual experiences the "existential slap"; the moment of realization of the imminence of one's death (Coyle, 2004). Considerations of dignity at the end of life require, first, an understanding of what is meant by dignity in dying, and, second, an understanding of how health care providers might not only preserve, but also augment dignity in this critical time. This paper seeks to provide conceptual clarity on what is meant by dying with dignity, present the profile of those at risk of having 'fractured dignity' and its consequences, and finally will present a model of dignity in the terminally ill and its clinical implications.

DYING WELL AND IDEAS OF DIGNITY

To die with dignity is a notion to which many of us subscribe, both professionally and personally. Indeed, the idea of dignity is evoked in our notions of a good death or dying well.

Both palliative care professional associations and research into defining quality care at the end of life speak to the goal of achieving dignified dying. The Canadian Hospice Palliative Care Association (CHPCA) (Ferris et al., 2002) and the World Health Organization's (WHO, 2002) definitions of palliative care capture a commitment to ensuring a death free of undue suffering or distress, attention to pain and symptom management, integration of psychological and spiritual care into daily care, support for patients to live as actively as possible until their death, and support for families throughout the patient's illness and into bereavement. Many of these ideas are echoed by the Institute of Medicine (1997), which defines a good death as "one that is free from avoidable distress and suffering for patients, families, and caregivers, in general accord with patients' and families' wishes, and reasonably consistent with clinical, cultural and ethical standards" (p. 24). Emanuel and Emanuel's (1998) model of a good death consists of eight modifiable dimensions, which encompass physical symptoms, social relationships and support, hopes and expectations, psychological and cognitive symptoms, economic demands and caregiving needs, and spiritual and existential beliefs. Research into the elements of quality care at the end of life echoes many of these domains of a good death (Mak & Clinton, 1999; Singer et al., 1999; Steinhauser et al., 2000).

Reflecting on these definitions, it appears that attending to the physical, psychological, spiritual and existential concerns of individuals with terminal illness is of paramount concern at the end of life. Several studies have illustrated that too frequently these needs go unmet, resulting in psychological distress and, for many, undue suffering (Abraham et al., 2006; Arnold et al., 2004, 2006; Morasso et al., 1999; Peters & Sellick, 2006). Oftentimes when such distress reaches a critical level, many patients feel they can no longer go on living. Chochinov and colleagues (1995) noted that 75% of patients who had a significant desire for hastening their death had moderate to severe pain compared to 46% of patients with mild to no pain. In the study of terminally ill patients with acquired immune deficiency syndrome (AIDS), Rosenfeld and colleagues (2000) identified that pain intensity was a significant predictor of desire for death in those who had pain. Similarly, Coyle and Sculco

(2004) identified uncontrolled pain as one of several antecedents preceding the expression of desire for a hastened death in patients with advanced cancer.

Other researchers have noted that depression contributes significantly to suicidal ideation in the terminally ill. Approximately 25% of all cancer patients will experience severe depressive symptoms; rates increase with increasing levels of pain, disability and advancing illness (Wilson et al., 2007a). In their literature review, Chochinov and Wilson (1995) report that clinical depression, poor pain control and lack of social support are significantly related to desires for hastened death, and that the degree of distress in these individuals is very high. In a more recent study examining depression and anxiety disorders in palliative care, Wilson and colleagues (2007a) identified that those who met the criteria for an anxiety or depressive disorder were significantly more likely to express a desire for death, report they were suffering and feel a loss of dignity. For many who experience depression, a profound sense of hopelessness exists (Breitbart et al., 2000; Duggleby, 2000; Jones et al., 2003). Desire for hastened death was noted by Breitbart and colleagues (2000) to be significantly related with clinical depression and hopelessness. This finding was noted by Chochinov et al. (1998) whereby hopelessness was highly correlated with suicidal ideation. A sense of hopelessness has been reported throughout the literature as a main reason many terminally ill patients would request a hastened death (Virik & Glare, 2002; Wilson et al., 2000, 2007a, b).

Evidence also points to a sense of self-perceived burden as a significant, troubling concern to many with terminal illness and that it is associated with psychological distress and notions of dignity (McPherson et al., 2007). Wilson and colleagues (2005a, b) have found that feeling a burden was more highly correlated with loss of dignity than with either physical symptoms or other social and psychological concerns. Indeed, self-perceived burden has emerged as a significant predictor of loss of dignity, with individuals reporting a fractured sense of dignity having a greater sense of burden and lower quality of life (Chochinov et al., 2005a). The finding that perceived burden is more highly correlated with psychological issues than physical problems has been noted by others (Chio et al., 2005; Cousineau et al., 2003). Often this feeling translates into requests for a hastened death, with physicians in one study reporting that 41 to 75% of requests for a hastened death are because the patients report feeling that they are a burden to others (McPherson et al., 2007). Of patients who had previously made a request for a hastened death, family members report 58 to 94% were distressed about being a burden to others (Ganzini et al., 2003; Morita et al., 2004). In Oregon, where physician-assisted suicide is legal, a strong sense of self-perceived burden was cited as a concern by 37% of patients who received a hastened death (Sullivan et al., 2001).

The picture that begins to emerge is that self-perceived burden, depression and hopelessness are intimately connected to one's notion of dignity and can be part of the existential distress experienced by some at the end of their life (McPherson et al., 2007). Kissane et al (2001) have attempted to capture this idea with their concept of demoralization syndrome in which the core feature consists of hopelessness, loss of meaning and existential distress—components whose antitheses are inherent in one's sense of dignity. When dignity is felt to be lost, terminally ill patients frequently feel they have no value, hope, purpose or meaning and as such often make requests for a hastened death (Chochinov et al., 1998; Wilson et al., 2007a). Coyle and Sculco (2004) in their phenomenological study of seven patients with advanced cancer found that often requests for an early death were made when the dying process was difficult, unendurable or done as a means to draw attention to their personhood beyond the disease process. Underlying this discussion is a sense that the self has become lost in the midst of dying and as a result one's dignity is overshadowed by one's suffering. These findings underscore the importance of delineating not only the factors that are responsible for an individual's sense of dignity, but also the factors that support or undermine a dying person's sense of dignity.

DEFINING DIGNITY

To date, the concept of dignity has been widely invoked in discussions regarding end-of-life care, yet few would argue that it is well understood. Dignity is a complex issue, which historically has been ambiguous in its interpretation and application. Some of this conceptual ambiguity arises from the intricate relationship between dignity and autonomy; often these terms are used synonymously (Pullman, 2004). In this regard, our sense of dignity is intimately tied to our ability to make rational choices, a position described by the 18th century philosopher Immanuel Kant (Pullman, 2004). However, several authors have questioned this idea as it implies that individuals who lack the capacity for autonomous decision-making, such as persons dying from Alzheimer's disease, also lack human dignity (Hawryluck, 2004; McClement & Chochinov, 2006).

To address such concerns, it may be helpful, as some authors have asserted, to think of dignity as two distinct but related concepts. The first, basic dignity or absolute dignity, is a universal concept and has been described as the intrinsic moral worth of all humans (Anderberg et al., 2007; Pullman, 2004). Personal dignity, on the other hand, refers to the socially constructed norms of the individual or subgroups of individuals (Pullman, 2004). Personal dignity is "individualistic, transient, and often tied to personal goals and social circumstances" (Chochinov, 2006). Similarly, Proulx and Jacelon's (2004) conception of dignity has both internal and external components. The inherent worth ascribed to all human beings is captured by the internal aspects of dignity, whereas external aspects of dignity are formulated by the subjective factors deemed important to the individual. These may include autonomy, meaningfulness, physical comfort, spirituality and interpersonal connectedness. Exploring further the concept of dignity with the focus on older people, Nordenfelt (2003, 2004) proposed four kinds of dignity:

- Dignity as merit includes the set of rights and honours bestowed through a person's rank in society that is either earned or inherited;
- Dignity as moral stature included respect of oneself as a moral human being and respect from others related to performances and attitudes and may vary in relation to own deeds;
- Dignity of personal identity focuses on issues of self-respect, including the concepts of integrity and autonomy;

- Dignity of 'Menschenwürde' (human rights) means that all humans have the same value and the same rights independent of gender, race, religion or age.

In light of these various conceptions, what emerges is a sense that dignity is a complex, multifaceted phenomenon—a concept that is socially constructed, individually perceived, embodied and relational (Street & Kissane, 2001). Dignity is thus rooted in our relationships with others, socially negotiated in our interactions and constructed through the telling or narrative of our life story (Coulehan, 2005; Leung, 2007).

Though these theoretical discussions of what comprises a sense of dignity are helpful, an understanding of the core components essential to a dying person's sense of dignity has been lacking. However, emerging research has begun to unpack this term, revealing some of the core domains of what comprises notions of dignity at the end of life.

EVIDENCE

To date, there has been a paucity of research exploring the concept of dignity at the end of life. Despite the limited quantity of information, this work helps to illuminate what dignity means for the dying individual. In Enes's (2003) qualitative study exploring the meaning of dignity from the perspectives of patients, relatives and health professionals in a hospice unit, dignity was composed of four main themes including being human in terms of having rights and being worthy of respect, having control, relationships and belonging, and maintaining the individual self. Often, ideas of dignity were shaped by social expectations and were affected by how an individual was treated; in this regard, professional attitudes had a profound effect on the dying person's dignity.

Pleschberger's (2007) grounded theory study of dignity and dying in nursing homes from the perspective of older nursing home residents stresses the importance of differentiating between dignity as an interpersonal concept and relational dignity. For many residents, their sense of relational dignity is formulated through their social relations and encounters, which can often be limited within this environment. The need for help and care were also seen as major threats to both interpersonal and relational dignity, in that older adults were afraid of becoming a burden. In this environment, dignity was most challenged by the threat of advancing illness and having care needs requiring assistance from others.

Street and Kissane's (2001) discourse analysis of the qualitative literature examining dignity in end-of-life care argues that our understanding of dignity is constructed through our relationships with others and is a subjective experience. Their work brings to light how dying individuals feel about their bodies and the care they receive at the end of their life. Indeed, the 'failure' of the body, whether conveyed through the smells of dying or bodily disintegration, can often lead to shame and disgust in the terminally ill, areas not often explored in the literature on dignity.

Over the last five years, the research group of Chochinov and colleagues has systematically explored the concept of dignity in the terminally ill. Their early research work sought to uncover the meaning of dignity and the factors related to this issue. Based on their qualitative study of 50 palliative cancer patients, an empirically derived model of dignity in the terminally ill was developed (Chochinov et al., 2002; Chochinov et al., 2002b). This model provides an understanding of the experiences that shape one's sense of dignity in light of a life-limiting illness and the ways in which dignity conserving care may be applied.

The Dignity Model suggests that an individual's perception of dignity is related to and influenced by three major areas: 1) illness-related concerns; 2) dignity-conserving repertoire; and 3) social dignity inventory. These categories capture the broad experiences and events that determine how individuals experience a sense of dignity at the end of life. Each category contains several themes and sub-themes, which further inform our understanding of dignity and the potential for therapeutic intervention.

Illness-related concerns are issues that derive from or are related to the illness itself and which threaten to or actually do hamper a patient's sense of dignity. As these concerns are mediated by the illness, they are very specific to the individual's experience of their life-limiting illness. The two themes subsumed in this category include "level of independence", which is determined by the ability to maintain one's cognitive and functional capacities. The second theme, "symptom distress," captures both the physical and psychological distress an individual may experience as a result of their illness. For many it is the intensity of physical symptoms that may affect their sense of dignity, whereas psychological distress captures the mental anguish brought about by not knowing, or being unaware of, aspects of their illness (medical uncertainty) and the worry or fear associated with one's impending death (death anxiety).

The social dignity inventory refers to those environmental factors external to the patient that may strengthen or undermine the quality of interactions with others and, thus, their sense of dignity. There are five externally mediated factors included in this category. The first, *privacy boundaries*, explains how dignity can be affected by encroachments on one's personal environment when receiving care or support. *Social support*, the second sub-theme, refers to the availability or presence of friends, family or health care providers who are perceived as helpful. Thirdly, *care tenor* is the attitude others demonstrate when providing care or interacting with the patient. The fourth sub-theme, *burden to others*, explores the distress patients experience when they either feel they are or fear they will become a burden to others as their personal care or management becomes more difficult for them to manage alone. Finally, *aftermath concerns* are those anticipated fears or worries that the impact of one's death will have on their loved ones.

Mediating these two categories, the patient's dignity-conserving repertoire consists of those internally held and socially mediated approaches the individual uses to maintain their sense of dignity. Consisting of two major themes—dignity-conserving perspectives and dignity-conserving practices—these areas incorporate aspects of a patient's psychological and spiritual views that may influence their sense of dignity. Dignity-conserving perspectives are the ways a patient perceives or copes with their current situation and includes eight sub-themes. Continuity of self is the sense that the core essence or identity of who one is remains intact despite progressing illness. Role preservation is the manner in which patients strive to maintain a sense of congruence with prior views of the self through one's ability to continue to function in usual roles. Generativity/legacy describes the comfort patients felt in knowing that their accomplishments, contributions and connections to life (e.g. children) would live on and be a testament of their life. The maintenance of pride speaks to the ability of patients facing death to maintain a personal sense of positive self-regard or self-respect. Seeing that life was not only enduring but also had meaning and purpose allowed patients to maintain a sense of hopefulness, and thus retain their dignity. Maintaining a sense of control or influence over life circumstances impacts a patient's sense of dignity, and in this regard the degree of autonomy a patient subjectively feels is of utmost importance. Acceptance is the ability to integrate and accommodate to life's changing circumstances. Finally, resilience/fighting spirit is a mental strategy some patients use to overcome their illness or to optimize their quality of life.

Dignity-conserving practices are the personal approaches or strategies that individuals use to improve or maintain their sense of dignity. These can include "living in the moment" whereby one focuses on immediate issues and future concerns are addressed; "maintaining normalcy" involves continuing with usual routines and schedules; and "seeking spiritual comfort" draws on previously held religious or spiritual beliefs in an attempt to find comfort.

To further explore the factors associated with one's sense of dignity, a cross-sectional cohort study of 213 terminally ill cancer patients being cared for either at home or at an in-patient palliative care facility was undertaken. Though most reported their dignity as intact, 53.5% of participants indicated they had great, some or occasional dignity concerns (Chochinov et al., 2002b). Those with a fractured sense of dignity (n=16, 7.5%) tended to be younger, be an in-patient, report more concerns with bowel functioning and changing appearance, and reported a higher desire for death and the loss of will to live. Additionally, those reporting intact dignity were less likely to report they felt depressed, hopeless or anxious. The strongest predictors of a fractured sense of dignity were deterioration in one's appearance, followed by a sense of being a burden to others, requiring assistance with bathing, presence of pain and location of care. Indeed, the issue of appearance or rather the perception of how patients believe themselves to be seen or appreciated by others, is of profound importance to many patients' sense of dignity. Thus, care providers must be aware that "the reflection patients see of themselves in the eye of the beholder" may affirm or detract from a patient's sense of dignity (Chochinov, 2004).

The salience of these findings was further tested using a factor analytic approach, which revealed six primary factors underlying a sense of dignity in the terminally ill (Hack et al., 2004). The six-factor solution accounted for 40.5% of the variance and describes unique aspects of the dying patients' experience: pain, intimate dependency, hopelessness/depression, informal support network, formal support network and quality of life. This factor structure closely approximates the model of dignity derived from previous qualitative work. Further regression modeling of the modifiable factors most significant to one's sense of dignity resulted in a highly significant two-factor model that included hopelessness/depression and intimate dependency needs. This model suggests that patients who report feeling depressed, and those who require assistance with aspects of personal care, such as toileting, transferring, dressing, bathing or are experiencing problems with continence, may be at higher risk of experiencing a loss of dignity.

The dignity model has been further validated by Chochinov et al. (2006), most recently with 211 cancer patients receiving palliative care either at home or on an in-patient specialty unit. Translating the themes and sub-themes of the model into 22 items, patients were asked to what extent they believed these specific issues were or could be related to their sense of dignity. Two items, "not feeling treated with respect or understanding" and "feeling a burden to others" were the issues most frequently endorsed as having an influence on their sense of dignity. These findings provide further evidence for the importance of patient self-perceptions as an important mediator of maintaining one's sense of dignity. Comparable to their previous finding, only 5.3% of the patients reported a sense of fractured dignity.

APPLICATION OF THE MODEL IN PRACTICE

The research literature to date and the model of dignity developed by Chochinov and colleagues (Chochinov, 2002; Chochinov et al., 2002a, b, 2006; Hack et al., 2004) helps to illuminate the key factors, issues and experiences that both bolster and hamper a dying patient's sense of dignity. From this knowledge, interventions aimed at restoring and improving dignity in the dying can be developed. For example, Doorenbos and colleagues' (2006) study with a sample of Indian nurses explored nursing actions in the three thematic areas of the model that facilitated dignified dying. They noted that the majority of dignity-conserving nursing interventions were aimed at promoting spiritual comfort, with the most important nursing actions to promote dignified dying centring on supporting spirituality at the end of life.

A more structured approach is a brief psychotherapeutic intervention called dignity therapy, developed and pilot tested by Chochinov and associates (Chochinov et al., 2004, 2005b). Grounded in the empirical model based on dying patients' self-reported ideas of dignity, dignity therapy combines elements from various psychotherapeutic traditions such as life review, logotherapy and existential psychotherapy. However, the focus of dignity therapy is to provide the patient the opportunity to discuss aspects of their life they feel most proud of, things they feel are or were most meaningful, the personal history they would want remembered, or even to provide instruction in the service of helping to look after their soon-to-be-bereft loved ones. These sessions are tape-recorded, transcribed, edited and returned to the patient thereby creating a tangible document that acknowledges the importance of generativity and legacy, in addition to augmenting the patient's sense of meaning and purpose.

Evidence suggests that patients who participate in this intervention report a heightened sense of dignity, an increased sense of purpose, a heightened sense of meaning and an increased will to live. Patients also reported that this intervention had helped or would help their family prepare for the future. These findings also resonate with the model developed by Coyle (2006), which describes the hard work cancer patients undertake when living in the face of death. The struggle to find meaning and create a legacy was of utmost importance to participants. Indeed, creating a legacy was a means to provide evidence of their value, significance and at times a justification for how they lived—all factors that resonate with a person's sense of dignity.

The unique aspect of the dignity model is that it provides clinicians with guidance and direction on how they may app-roach dignity concerns, even through less structured approaches than interventions such as dignity therapy (McClement et al., 2004). In this manner, the clinician can use the themes and sub-themes of the dignity model as a jumping-off point to initiate conversations with patients as to what may be of importance to them. For example, a nurse, when conducting the admission procedure to a hospice unit, might want to not only ask the standard questions about a patient's illness, but also to explore what they feel passionately about, for instance relationships, religious or spiritual beliefs, vocation or even hobbies. In this manner a fuller understanding of who the person is can be obtained and activities to support role preservation can be proposed; for instance, an elderly gentleman who had worked in remote northern Aboriginal communities was offered help in arranging a sweet-grass ceremony as a way of connecting with his spiritual self and helping him to prepare for death. Without knowing what matters to individuals, it is impossible to anticipate or accommodate the various things that might reinforce their sense of personhood and help maintain a sense of dignity until the very end.

The model also helps to clue health care providers into aspects of themselves they bring to the bedside, which may impede or foster patient dignity. Adapting the simple A, B, C, D mnemonic, Chochinov (2007) provides guidance for health care providers in ways they can affirm a patient's value and provide dignity-conserving care. Within this paradigm, "A", or attitude, requires clinicians to examine their attitudes and assumptions towards patients. This personal assessment is geared towards gaining an understanding of how our interactions in the clinical setting are shaped by our internal belief systems. The importance of this reflection cannot be understated, as previous research has provided evidence that patients look to clinicians as a barometer of their sense of worth, and seek from them some form of self-affirmation (Chochinov et al., 2002; Jacobsen, 2007).

The "B", or behaviour, derives from our attitudes towards patients. Awareness that one's behaviour can mediate sense of dignity requires that clinicians always respond in ways that convey respect and kindness when interacting with patients. Compassion, the "C" of the paradigm, reflects an awareness of the suffering of another human being along with the desire to alleviate it. Compassion arrives in different ways to different people—for some it can be intuitive, for some, acquired by way of life experience. For others, compassion accumulates through clinical practice or is cultivated through the study of humanities, arts, social sciences and ethics. It is recognized that compassion can be conveyed by our words as well as our actions. This further attests to the need for an awareness of our approach to patients in the clinical setting. Finally "D", or dialogue, is a critical element of dignity-conserving care. At the core of this domain, clinicians must communicate information and discuss treatment options, but do so in the context of conversations that acquaint them with aspects that define who the person is, in other words, taking the time to acknowledge the personhood of an individual beyond their illness.

CONCLUSION

Facilitating dignified dying is an altruistic goal of many in the palliative care profession. Until recently, there was little guidance from the research literature on how a patient's dignity might be preserved or augmented during the dying process. The research conducted by Chochinov and colleagues provides a framework for understanding the notion of dignity, the issues that might be of importance to people facing a life-limiting illness, and strategies to provide dignity-conserving care. Though this body of research literature sheds light on our understanding of dignity in the terminally ill, future work must extend to testing the model and dignity-conserving interventions in populations dying from diseases other than cancer, such as congestive heart failure, chronic obstructive lung disease and the frail elderly— diseases whose illness trajectories often present great uncertainty and disability near the end of life. Regardless of the disease process, health care professionals must be mindful of the presence they bring to the clinical encounter, as patients' notions of dignity are intimately tied to and formulated by the reflection they see of themselves in those who provide them care.

REFERENCES

Abraham, A., Kutner, J. S. & Beaty, B. (2006). Suffering at the end of life in the setting of low physical symptom distress. *Journal of Palliative Medicine, 9*(3), 658-65.

Anderberg, P., Lepp, M., Berglund, A.L. & Segesten, K. (2007). Preserving dignity in caring for older adults: A concept analysis. *Journal of Advanced Nursing, 59*(6), 635-43.

Arnold, E.M., Artin, K.A., Griffith, D., Person, J.L. & Graham, K.G. (2006). Unmet needs at the end of life: Perceptions of hospice social workers. *Journal of Social Work in End-of-Life & Palliative Care, 2*(4), 61-83.

Arnold, E.M., Artin, K.A., Person, J.L. & Griffith, D.L. (2004). Consideration of hastening death among hospice patients and their families. *Journal of Pain and Symptom Management, 27*(6), 523-32.

Breitbart, W., Rosenfeld, B., Pessin, H., Kaim, M., Funesti-Esch, J., Galietta, M. et al. (2000). Depression, hopelessness, and desire for hastened death in terminally ill patients with cancer. *JAMA: Journal of the American Medical Association, 284*(22), 2907-11.

Chio, A., Gauthier, A., Calvo, A., Ghiglione, P. & Mutani, R. (2005). Caregiver burden and patients' perception of being a burden in ALS. *Neurology, 64*(10), 1780-82.

Chochinov, H.M. (2002). Dignity-conserving care—a new model for palliative care: Helping the patient feel valued. *JAMA: Journal of the American Medical Association, 287*(17), 2253-60.

Chochinov, H.M. (2004). Dignity and the eye of the beholder. *Journal of Clinical Oncology, 22*(7), 1336-40.

Chochinov, H.M. (2006). Dying, dignity, and new horizons in palliative end-of-life care. *CA: A Cancer Journal for Clinicians, 56*(2), 84-103.

Chochinov, H.M. (2007). Dignity and the essence of medicine: The A, B, C & D of dignity-conserving care. *British Medical Journal, 335,* 184-87.

Chochinov, H.M., Hack, T., Hassard, T., Kristjanson, L.J., McClement, S. & Harlos, M. (2002a). Dignity in the terminally ill: A cross-sectional, cohort study. *Lancet, 360*(9350), 2026-30.

Chochinov, H.M., Hack, T., McClement, S., Kristjanson, L. & Harlos, M. (2002b). Dignity in the terminally ill: A developing empirical model. *Social Science & Medicine (1982), 54*(3), 433-43.

Chochinov, H.M., Hack, T., Hassard, T., Kristjanson, L.J., McClement, S. & Harlos, M. (2004). Dignity and psychotherapeutic considerations in end-of-life care. *Journal of Palliative Care, 20*(3), 134-42.

Chochinov, H.M., Hack, T., Hassard, T., Kristjanson, L.J., McClement, S. & Harlos, M. (2005). Dignity therapy: A novel psychotherapeutic intervention for patients near the end of life. *Journal of Clinical Oncology, 23*(24), 5520-25.

Chochinov, H.M., Krisjanson, L.J., Hack, T.F., Hassard, T., McClement, S. & Harlos, M. (2006). Dignity in the terminally ill: Revisited. *Journal of Palliative Medicine, 9*(3), 666-72.

Chochinov, H.M. & Wilson, K.G. (1995a). The euthanasia debate: Attitudes, practices and psychiatric considerations. *Canadian Journal of Psychiatry. Revue Canadienne de Psychiatrie, 40*(10), 593-602.

Chochinov, H.M., Wilson, K.G., Enns, M., Mowchun, N., Lander, S., Levitt, M. et al. (1995b). Desire for death in the terminally ill. *American Journal of Psychiatry, 152*(8), 1185-91.

Chochinov, H.M., Wilson, K.G., Enns, M. & Lander, S. (1998). Depression, hopelessness, and suicidal ideation in the terminally ill. *Psychosomatics, 39*(4), 366-70.

Coulehan, J. (2005). 'They wouldn't pay attention': Death without dignity. *American Journal of Hospice & Palliative Care, 22*(5), 339-43.

Cousineau, N., McDowell, I., Hotz, S. & Hebert, P. (2003). Measuring chronic patients' feelings of being a burden to their caregivers: Development and preliminary validation of a scale. *Medical Care, 41*(1), 110-18.

Coyle, N. (2004). The existential slap—a crisis of disclosure. *International Journal of Palliative Nursing, 10*(11), 520.

Coyle, N. (2006). The hard work of living in the face of death. *Journal of Pain and Symptom Management, 32*(3), 266-74.

Coyle, N. & Sculco, L. (2004). Expressed desire for hastened death in seven patients living with advanced cancer: A phenomenologic inquiry. *Oncology Nursing Forum, 31*(4), 699-709.

Doorenbos, A.Z., Wilson, S.A., Coenen, A. & Borse, N.N. (2006). Dignified dying: Phenomenon and actions among nurses in India. *International Nursing Review, 53*(1), 28-33.

Duggleby, W. (2000). Enduring suffering: A grounded theory analysis of the pain experience of elderly hospice patients with cancer. *Oncology Nursing Forum, 27*(5), 825-31.

Emanuel, E.J. & Emanuel, L.L. (1998). The promise of a good death. *Lancet, 351*(Suppl 2), SII21-SII29.

Enes, S.P. (2003). An exploration of dignity in palliative care. *Palliative Medicine, 17*(3), 263-69.

Ferris, F.D., Balfour, H.M., Bowen, K., Farley, J., Hardwick, M., Lamontagne, C. et al. (2002). *A model to guide hospice palliative care.* Ottawa, ON: Canadian Hospice Palliative Care Association.

Ganzini, L., Dobscha, S., Heintz, R. & Press, N. (2003). Oregon physicians' perceptions of patients who request assisted suicide and their families. *Journal of Palliative Medicine, 6*(3), 381-90.

Hack, T.F., Chochinov, H.M., Hassard, T., Kristjanson, L.J., McClement, S. & Harlos, M. (2004). Defining dignity in terminally ill cancer patients: A factor-analytic approach. *Psycho Oncology, 13*(10), 700-08.

Haddock, J. (1996). Towards further clarification of the concept 'dignity'. *Journal of Advanced Nursing, 24*(5), 924-31.

Hawryluck, L. (2004). Lost in translation: Dignity dialogues at the end of life. *Journal of Palliative Care, 20*(3), 150-54.

Institute of Medicine. (1997). In J.M. Field & C.K. Cassel (Eds.), *Approaching death: Improving care at the end of life*. Washington, DC: National Academy Press.

Jacelon, C.S., Connelly, T.W., Brown, R., Proulx, K. & Vo, T. (2004). A concept analysis of dignity for older adults. *Journal of Advanced Nursing, 48*(1), 76-83.

Jacobsen, N. (2007). Dignity and health: A review. *Social Science & Medicine, 64*(2), 292-302.

Jones, J.M., Huggins, M.A., Rydall, A.C. & Rodin, G.M. (2003). Symptomatic distress, hopelessness, and the desire for hastened death in hospitalized cancer patients. *Journal of Psychosomatic Research, 55*(5), 411-18.

Kissane, D.W., Clarke, D.M. & Street, A.F. (2001). Demoralization syndrome—a relevant psychiatric diagnosis for palliative care. *Journal of Palliative Care, 17*(1), 12-21.

Leung, D. (2007). Granting death with dignity: Patient, family and professional perspectives. *International Journal of Palliative Nursing, 13*(4), 170-74.

Mak, J.M. & Clinton, M. (1999). Promoting a good death: An agenda for outcomes research—a review of the literature. *Nursing Ethics, 6*(2), 97-106.

McClement, S.E. & Chochinov, H.M. (2006). Dignity in palliative care. In E. Bruera, I. Higginson, C. von Gunten & C. Ripamonti (Eds.), *Textbook of palliative medicine* (pp. 100-07). New York: Edward Arnold.

McClement, S.E., Chochinov, H.M., Hack, T.F., Kristjanson, L.J. & Harlos, M. (2004). Dignity-conserving care: Application of research findings to practice. *International Journal of Palliative Nursing, 10*(4), 173-79.

McPherson, C.J., Wilson, K.G. & Murray, M.A. (2007). Feeling like a burden: Exploring the perspectives of patients at the end of life. *Social Science & Medicine (1982), 64*(2), 417-27.

Morasso, G., Capelli, M., Viterbori, P., Di Leo, S., Alberisio, A., Costantini, M. et al. (1999). Psychological and symptom distress in terminal cancer patients with met and unmet needs. *Journal of Pain and Symptom Management, 17*(6), 402-09.

Dying with Dignity:
A Contemporary Challenge in End-of-Life Care

Morita, T., Kawa, M., Honke, Y., Kohara, H., Maeyama, E., Kizawa, Y. et al. (2004). Existential concerns of terminally ill cancer patients receiving specialized palliative care in Japan. *Supportive Care in Cancer, 12*(2), 137-40.

Nordenfelt, L. (2003). Dignity and the care of the elderly. *Medicine, Health Care, and Philosophy, 6*(2), 103-10.

Nordenfelt, L. (2004). The varieties of dignity. *Health Care Analysis, 12*(2), 69-81; discussion 83-89.

Peters, L. & Sellick, K. (2006). Quality of life of cancer patients receiving inpatient and home-based palliative care. *Journal of Advanced Nursing, 53*(5), 524-33.

Pleschberger, S. (2007). Dignity and the challenge of dying in nursing homes: The residents' view. *Age and Ageing, 36*(2), 197-202.

Pullman, D. (2004). Death, dignity, and moral nonsense. *Journal of Palliative Care, 20*(3), 171-78.

Proulx, K. & Jacelon, C.S. (2004). Dying with dignity: The good patient versus the good death. American. *Journal of Hospice and Palliative Care, 22*(2), 116-20.

Rosenfeld, B., Breitbart, W., Galietta, M., Kaim, M., Funesti-Esch, J., Pessin, H. et al. (2000). The schedule of attitudes toward hastened death: Measuring desire for death in terminally ill cancer patients. *Cancer, 88*(12), 2868-75.

Singer, P.A., Martin, D.K. & Kelner, M. (1999). Quality end-of-life care: Patients' perspectives. *JAMA: Journal of the American Medical Association, 281*(2), 163-68.

Steinhauser, K.E., Clipp, E.C., McNeilly, M., Christakis, N.A., McIntyre, L.M. & Tulsky, J.A. (2000). In search of a good death: Observations of patients, families, and providers. *Annals of Internal Medicine, 132*(10), 825-32.

Street, A.F. & Kissane, D.W. (2001). Constructions of dignity in end-of-life care. *Journal of Palliative Care, 17*(2), 93-101.

Sullivan, A.D., Hedberg, K. & Hopkins, D. (2001). Legalized physician-assisted suicide in Oregon, 1998-2000. *New England Journal of Medicine, 344*(8), 605-07.

Virik, K. & Glare, P. (2002). Requests for euthanasia made to a tertiary referral teaching hospital in Sydney, Australia, in the year 2000. *Supportive Care in Cancer, 10*(4), 309-13.

WHO. (2002). *World Health Organization definition of palliative care*, 2006: http://www.who.int.proxy2.lib.umanitoba.ca/cancer/palliative/definition/en/

Wilson, K.G., Chochinov, H.M., de Faye, B.J. & Breitbart, W. (2000). Diagnosis and management of depression in palliative care. In H.M. Chochinov & W. Breitbart (Eds.), *Handbook of psychiatry in palliative medicine* (1st ed., pp. 25-49). New York: Oxford University Press.

Wilson, K.G., Chochinov, H.M., Skirko, M.G., Allard, P., Chary, S., Gagnon, P.R. et al. (2007a). Depression and anxiety disorders in palliative cancer care. *Journal of Pain and Symptom Management, 33*(2), 118-29.

Wilson, K.G., Chochinov, H.M., McPherson, C.J., Skirko, M.G., Allard, P., Chary, S. et al. (2007b). Desire for euthanasia or physician-assisted suicide in palliative cancer care. *Health Psychology, 26*(3), 314-23.

Wilson, K.G., Curran, D. & McPherson, C.J. (2005). A burden to others: A common source of distress for the terminally ill. *Cognitive Behaviour Therapy, 34*(2), 115-23.

5

The Ends of Life:
Public Policy, Reason and Faith
Part 1 ~ Notes on the Ends of Life

Allan E. Blakeney, QC, OC, FRSC

Former Premier of Saskatchewan,
Visiting Scholar, University of Saskatchewan College of Law

I thank the organizers for giving me the opportunity to be part of this intriguing series of lectures on death and dying and particularly on the role of second parties in death and dying.

Why is this a topic of increasing interest? There are several contributing factors. With easier working lives, fewer devastating wars, and advances in nutrition and medicine we as a nation are living longer. But advances are not even. (We envy the one-hoss shay when all parts collapsed at the same instant. Not so, humans). So we are often able to prolong life without being able to prolong well-being. There is a sharp increase in degenerative diseases (cancer, diabetes and the like) as causes of death. And that has caused us to think.

Those of us of mature years are all too familiar with how these developments have shaped our lives. Our conversations are filled with lamentations about ailments, treatments and pills. We have pills for every ailment known and pills for ailments not previously known: the AB syndrome or the XY dysfunction.

As my ninth decade "progresses", if that is the appropriate word, I am becoming increasingly a part of these conversations. We commiserate with each other and end by saying that growing old is not for sissies. And then comfort each other by repeating the bromide "well, it's better than the alternative." And we accept that as a given. But lately more of us are thinking, "Perhaps we're being a bit hasty in that judgement. Maybe death has more to be said in its favour than we have recognized.

Perhaps we should consider the pros and cons of a death that we have helped along. Give death a chance, as it were." And that, I believe, is what this lecture series is attempting to do—not give death a chance but rather consider the pros and cons of a death we have helped along.

In this series of lectures, you have heard from people who are well informed about the medical, the legal and other aspects of the issue. I am asked to speak about the public policy issues that surround death and dying and particularly death that is in some way aided or abetted by some person other than the dear departed or soon to be departed.

We have decided to have two relatively short presentations. I felt that I could either talk about the substance of such issues or the approach that politicians take to such issues, but not both. What I propose to do is to approach the whole area through the eyes of a politician.

What do we mean by public policy issues? Well, we live in a pluralistic society. By that I mean that people have a wide range of opinions and beliefs based on different ethnic backgrounds, religions, secular beliefs and ages. And we live in a democratic society, broadly defined. This means that the laws that govern our lives should be widely acceptable to a very large majority of citizens. Otherwise it is very difficult to create and maintain social cohesion and social harmony, particularly in a society as pluralistic as ours.

We elect governments—federal, provincial and local. These governments perform two broad functions: 1) they raise money and they spend it on things we think we can do better together than we can separately and 2) they make rules and they enforce them. Governments do a few other things like encapsulating our sense of nationhood—what are queens and governors-general for?

But with respect to death and dying we are chiefly concerned with making rules and enforcing them. So, governments make all kinds of rules on all kinds of subjects—what's the problem with death and dying?

There are a couple of problems that are special to issues like death and dying. I want to deal with two.

In this area, what should be the function of the laws we make? Given that society works best if our laws are acceptable to a large majority of the public, how do we achieve the consensus or the compromise that allows laws on assisted death and dying to be widely acceptable? I want to touch on these two issues: function and compromise.

FUNCTION

I turn to the first issue: function. What do we want our laws to do? I'm always surprised and sometimes amused at public expectations of their political leaders and political processes. Politics is an activity where leaders are called upon to seek support and approval from people of widely differing opinions and beliefs. Except on narrow issues, there is rarely a majority opinion. There is simply a cluster of minorities. This is not conducive to leaders showing complete candour and transparency. Most will try to avoid falsehoods, but a certain reticence with the whole truth is usually required. Yet many people somehow expect their political leaders to be moral leaders.

You ask, what has this got to do with death and dying? The same mindset leads many people to believe that our laws should embody our moral principles. One of the Ten Commandments of Moses says: "thou shalt not commit adultery". And not so long ago in many jurisdictions in North America adultery was indeed a crime. There were rarely prosecutions and even more rarely convictions. But it proved difficult indeed to get those laws off the books, because they embodied moral precepts that we accepted in principle, although often not in practice. We simply did not wish to acknowledge in a public way that this principle was not a workable rule for civil society.

Lest you feel that this strange approach to law-making is confined to distant places, recall that the advertising and promotion of birth control medicines and devices was illegal in all of Canada until 1969, less than 40 years ago. This was a law not because it was felt necessary to promote social cohesion but because it embodied a moral or perhaps a religious precept now or formerly embraced by a large number of people.

I say "now or formerly" to make the point that these laws often linger on the statute books long after support for them has waned. When the law was repealed, the Conference of Catholic Bishops said they did not oppose repeal. They counselled their parishioners against birth control devices, but acknowledged that in a pluralistic society other views were possible—an approach I commend to all of us.

If you doubt this portrayal of the public's position on the function of laws, consider the recent debate on legalizing same-sex marriage. Overwhelmingly, the opposition to the change of the law was framed, not in terms of whether the prohibition against gay marriage was necessary to allow our pluralistic society to live together, but rather that it was needed to set out important values that are, or should be, at the core of our society—not a "working rule test" but rather a "statement of core values test".

The public continues to want the law both to set out our workable rules and to embody moral principles and values. And that is often tough to accomplish.

COMPROMISE

I turn to the second issue—compromise—and how to achieve a compromise that will allow a law to be acceptable to a large majority of the public.

When governments make a rule they usually try to make one that a large majority of the public will accept. If, on a particular issue, 40% of the people feel strongly one way and 35% feel strongly in an opposite direction and 25% favour some-thing in the middle, the best rule is probably the one favoured by the 25% because a large block of the 40% and the 35% can probably acquiesce in the compromise. They can live with it and we have a workable rule; not many are happy but, more importantly, not many are desperately unhappy.

I've oversimplified, but this is the art of statecraft. As an aside it will be seen that, in my judgement, the wrong way to make rules is to set out a question and ask what percentage favour a yes or no answer and make the rule accordingly. This binary view of governance creates streams of winners and losers and makes compromise positions harder to find. Equally impor-tant, it makes citizens feel that citizenship is a game of winners and losers rather than an exercise in learning to get along with our fellow citizens in a pluralistic society.

But I am straying a bit. Issues of death and dying are very difficult to get people to compromise on. In the minds of many there are so few half-way positions. That is partly because we do not agree on what we are talking about.

There is widespread agreement about the biological facts about birth and death. We generally agree that medical people can tell us when a child has been conceived and when it is born. Similarly, although not quite so clearly, we agree when a person is physically dead. When the heart and circulatory system stops operating and when the lungs stop functioning a person is dead.

The biological facts are reasonably clear. The theological facts are far from clear, because there is no general agreement on what a human being is. There is widespread agreement that we are animals—vertebrates, primates and we have a gene composition surprisingly like some other primates. But there is a very widely held view that we are something more. That we consist of body and soul or perhaps body, mind and spirit. Soul, spirit—what is this all about?

We note that through the course of the last 5,000 or 10,000 years of human history, that mankind (and may I use the term as meaning humanity in a non-gender sense) mankind has come to believe there is something more. This is not only the result of asking questions about how we got here, about prime cause—questions that are totally unanswerable. They come as a result of us developing a sense of moral and ethical values like compassion, altruism, mercy.

Are these the directions of a power external to us, one which we call God? Or are they a body of non-empirical beliefs or truths that mankind is developing, evolving—what I choose to call a spiritual universe, and we call them God?

To paraphrase, I believe, George Bernard Shaw: Is mankind the greatest creation of God or is God the greatest creation of mankind and does it matter? I don't propose to dispose of these simple questions in the course of a 20-minute lecture.

I raise them because they shape the views that citizens hold about the nature of human life. Many views are held, but let me set out two, which I hope are representative:

1. There is a deity—omnipotent, omniscient and ever-present. He/she sees each sparrow fall. At the conception of each human child the deity endows the body with a soul. The soul takes on the individual attributes of that person. At death (or

perhaps sometime later) that soul leaves the body and joins other departed souls in heaven, in paradise, in the realm of the deity. We see this view articulated every day in an obituary notice "John James has gone to join his wife who predeceased him in 2002 and one son who passed away in 2005." Or in a hymn: "God be with you 'til we meet again – 'Til we meet, 'til we meet, 'til we meet at Jesus' feet".

That is one view. Another is:

2. We are born as primates with the potential to become fully human. We develop a sense of right and wrong, of our obligation to our fellow humans, and become part of the spiritual universe created by our forebears. We develop an individual soul and through our lifetime make our contribution. Upon death our individual soul dies with our body. Our claim to eternity is as part of the continuing spiritual universe (using my term). As an *individual* we exist only in memory, in the individual memory of those who survive us as earthlings and as may be recorded in the conscious or unconscious memory of mankind as it shapes its sense of the divine.

I outline these two views. You could state others. But these are reasonable representations of two broad streams of opinion. And these views very often engender sharply different reactions to public policy issues of death and dying.

Note that empirical evidence—evidence we gain from our senses or from logical deductions from that evidence—is absent from both views. Those charged with the job of shaping public policy are well aware of the fact that views like these are held and held strongly as truth.

Let me turn to considering suicide, euthanasia and assisted suicide. Even unassisted suicide is not free from difficulty. The view that each human is given a soul at conception by the deity and it is up to the deity to decide when it is to be called home was widely held. Suicide was a crime under the Criminal Code of Canada until 1972. It no longer is. But the action of assisting a person to commit suicide remains a crime under the Canadian Criminal Code. A new section was added to make this so. What's going on here?

Some oppose the legalization of assisted suicide because they fear that it would be abused, that people whose existence was inconvenient would be pressured by others to consent to suicide and then would be assisted to complete the termination of life. And that is a legitimate concern. This view is often put forward by people who are advocates for the rights of disabled people. They have fought a long fight to get the rights of disabled people recognized by society and our laws, and they see the legalization of assisted suicide as a threat to the gains they have achieved.

But, that is not all that is going on. Where it is clear that a person of sound mind makes a rational decision to commit suicide and is unable to do so because of physical disability, that person cannot legally get a friend to assist them. That, I think, is a fair interpretation of the Sue Rodriguez case decided by the Supreme Court of Canada in 1993.

You will recall that Sue Rodriguez was the woman in British Columbia who was suffering from A.L.S.—Lou Gehrig's disease—and was totally disabled. She wished to commit suicide and she claimed that she had a right to have someone to help her. Her argument was that if she was able-bodied she could easily and legally commit suicide. But since she was disabled and couldn't manage it herself she had a right to help. To deny her that help was to discriminate against her because of her disability, contrary to the Charter of Rights adopted in 1982.

She launched a legal action to establish her right. The case eventually went to the Supreme Court of Canada who rejected her "right" by a vote of five judges to four.

So, why doesn't Parliament deal with this? I believe it is because there are still many people who believe that suicide is immoral because the perpetrator is usurping the function of the deity. The deity should decide when life ends and the soul returns home, not you or me. And this has been made part of the core doctrine of some religious organizations. Certainly there are other arguments. But it seems to me that while we grudgingly concede that a person may have a "right" to commit suicide, we claim, on some ground, that nobody has the "right" to help him.

In circumstances like these, what will the policy makers do? In these cases there will be a tendency to allow public opinion to shape and to jell. That is what the Sue Rodriguez case was all about—to try to shape public opinion to the other view—"Who's life is it, anyway? It is my life and if I am fully competent to make the judgement to end my life, and if I make the judgement, then it is no business of the state to interfere". Similar arguments arise with respect to euthanasia. It is hard to talk about this since there is a thicket of definitions:

Voluntary euthanasia: where the patient has requested or agreed to be dispatched.

Non-voluntary: where the patient has not given such clear indications of his/her desires.

Involuntary: where the patient has indicated that he/she does not want to die.

Involuntary is easy. This is against the law and will clearly remain so. The difficulties arise with voluntary euthanasia and non-voluntary euthanasia. Voluntary euthanasia is where the patient has made his or her wishes clear in favour of euthanasia. But that is still illegal. The Sue Rodriguez case was such an example.

Non-voluntary euthanasia arises where, for example, a patient is terminally ill and in great pain and where (say) a doctor administers morphine to kill the pain knowing that it will very possibly kill the patient.

Some of us believe that society could come up with safeguards to prevent abuse of the voluntary and non-voluntary euthanasia. This has been done in Holland and Oregon.

Some believe that there is more at play here than we are prepared to admit. Some believe that it is just not the job of the state to allow one person to take the life of another. That should be left to the cosmic plan.

And these are tough issues to argue for or against because the bases for the beliefs are not fundamentally based on logic. In a very well written and closely argued book, Professor Jocelyn Downie makes the point that, at the patient's insistence, it is perfectly legal to turn off a respirator so that the patient will certainly die. But if the patient asks for an injection of (say) potassium chloride to stop his heart functioning so that the patient will certainly die, that is illegal. She argues that this position does not make logical sense or ethical sense. And she is probably right.

But the public is often not logical. If most people are comfortable with a disconnected respirator but uncomfortable with potassium chloride then, however illogical, policy makers will have a strong tendency to respect the public sense of right and wrong.

A distinguished American judge, Oliver Wendell Holmes Jr., said "the life of the law is not in logic but in experience". By the same token I would say that very often the life of public policy is not in logic but in experience.

But public opinion changes. The Supreme Court of Canada does not agree that our Constitution in its Charter of Rights and Freedoms allows a disabled person to be assisted to commit suicide. But four of the nine judges of the Court agreed. The Canadian Medical Association, in its official position, is comfortable with the disconnected respirator but not with potassium chloride. But I suspect that all of these bodies will change their position as experience from Holland, Oregon and the many unofficial cases of assisted suicide and euthanasia, in the guise of palliative care, become part of the thinking of doctors, as I believe it is becoming. And that is where we are with laws that prohibit assisting some persons to commit suicide and which prohibit euthanasia of terminally ill persons by medical practitioners in order to end their life and so end their acute suffering.

We are now in the process of changing those laws slowly. At this stage we are not ready to make any formal change in the law. We are changing the law by changing the way we enforce them. In fact very few physicians are ever prosecuted for hastening the death of terminally ill, suffering patients. It would be better if we set out to change the laws in a formal way. This would force public discussion about both of the main issues as I see them: function and compromise.

CONCLUSION

There are some very important values at stake: the value of the sanctity of life; the value of the right of every person to autonomy and self-determination; the value of the right of every person to dignity; and differences in the public mind about the rank order of these values; differences which arise out of differences of belief about the nature of the universe and the place of humans in it; the existence and nature of God and the human soul, and our identity.

These are matters not to be settled by logical argument, although logical arguments should be brought to bear, and are. Policy makers seek to find answers that will be acceptable not because of the cogency of the reasoning but because they respond to the deeply held and, regrettably, very different beliefs among citizens of our very diverse society.

 6

The Ends of Life:
Public Policy, Reason and Faith
Part 2 ~ A Theological Contribution

The Reverend Canon Eric Beresford
BSc, BA, MA, DD (honoris causa)
President, Atlantic School of Theology

Stanley Hauerwas tells us "It is the worst of times to be a Christian theologian; it is the best of times." And the reason that both of these claims are true is that most people in our culture and time could not give a damn. Theology is a marginal activity, quite literally an activity on the margins of our cultural life, with little relevance for its day-to-day activities, and that, many would argue, is how it should be. Nowhere is this truer than in the area of public policy formation. The attempt to shape public policy in controversial areas is a thankless one at the best of times, but in areas where religious passions become engaged—areas like euthanasia and physician-assisted suicide—public policy formation pretty quickly becomes bogged down in claim and counter-claim, and the energy of the debate seems doomed to produce rather more heat than light. Yet is this really the result of the attempt to import narrowly religious concerns into a public debate that needs to be based on more generally shared, more rational grounds, or does the problem run wider?

In what follows, I do not intend to give a religious argument for or against the legalization of physician-assisted suicide and euthanasia. The question that I have been asked to address is a much more fundamental question, which I take to be about the role of religiously motivated insights and arguments in public debate in a pluralistic society such as ours.

You will note that I did not say in a secular society, and you might wonder why. Actually, there are a number of reasons.

First, the term secular is one that has religious origins. It is derived from the Latin *saeculum* a term that initially referred to that which belonged to this age, as opposed to what was to be understood, *sub specie aeterni* (from the perspective of eternity). In its roots then, the secular is a derivative concept. Of course, that is not how it is used now, but part of the problem is that the way it is used currently is riddled with ambiguities. Are we referring to a society or context from which religious faith is absent? Are we referring to one in which religious faith is excluded from public discourse, or merely one that does not privilege one particular religious perspective? A society in which there is a separation of church and state? These are all different ways in which the term secular is used, but I want to start by suggesting that the word pluralism provides a better description of the Canadian context than the word secular.

This is not to deny that certain aspects of religious faith are rather less common now than they were at previous points in our history. The decline in religious practice since the 1950s has been well documented. At the same time, religious *belief* continues to be an important dimension of the life of many Canadians, and if for most this does not translate into allegiance to particular religious institutions, the importance that people ascribe to their religious beliefs should not be underestimated. What has changed markedly over that period of time is the diversity of religious beliefs and practices that shape the lives of Canadians. According to census after census, religious faith is alive and well in Canada. It is just taking increasingly diverse forms.[191] These religious believers are all part of Canadian society, whose character turns out, therefore, to be pluralistic rather than simply secular.

By contrast, the language of the secular is often used to oppose those of religious faith to the wider culture in ways that presume the homogeneity and objectivity of the wider culture

---

[191] It is perhaps worth noting that this is not the first period in history in which a disjunction between religious faith and religious practice can be seen. Although the Middle Ages in England were undeniably religious, there is considerable evidence that participation in liturgies was quite limited. Further, this appears to be true of such regular rituals as the weekly or daily mass, and of life markers such as marriage. In pre-modern England it was not uncommon to live together without benefit of marriage.

and reduces churches and other religious institutions to special interest groups. This elides the contribution of religious faith to society and even to secularity. For instance, we should not underestimate the contributions that religion has made to the shaping of society. Even on matters where religious believers tend to be critical, there have been significant contributions. For example, the easy targets for the churches (and I will speak mostly from that context since it is the one I know best) are individualism and consumerism. Yet it is easy to forget that at least one historical account of the rise of individualism traces it to theologically motivated concerns for human dignity, and the claims of conscience and of religious liberty. It was, after all, Aquinas who framed the dictum *conscientia semper sequenda* (conscience ought always be followed). Similarly, consumerism is not unrelated to the values that arose in early modern capitalism, values that were linked famously by Weber to the Protestant work ethic.

Actually, in the debates around euthanasia there is a quite startling degree of agreement between protagonists on all sides. We all agree, publicly at least, that human dignity needs to be protected and the individual freedom to choose how to confront finitude and death must be preserved. We, for the most part, agree that life is one of the highest goods, but not an ultimate good, to be preserved at all costs. We all recognize that in relationship to death and dying there can be situations in which the good of physical life comes into conflict with other goods that we see as being served by our lives if they are to be at all meaningful. We all feel compassion towards those who suffer near death and would wish to see that suffering minimized or, if possible, ended. The difficulty is that we, each of us, understand different things by these goods, we draw different conclusions from them and we balance them differently. And underlying our differences there are, even for supposedly secular commentators, subtle differences in the way we understand human life in community, its ends and its purposes.

In understanding the "ends of life" the challenge is not religion, which has through its history been cast as an interminable series of argument and counter argument. It is not simply religious groups that stand in the way of what some see as rational progress in this area (and not all religious groups do stand in the way). There have also been significant advocacy efforts from groups representing the elderly and the disabled. These advocacy efforts are not simply based on ungrounded fear or misunderstandings of the data; rather they are rooted in different understandings of the value and purpose of human life and different experiences of disability and difference, and different encounters with the proximity of our own death.

So let me turn to ethics. The first thing I want to note is that theological reflection has, in fact, contributed significantly to the shaping of the content, the methods and the practices of bioethics. It was theology that set ethics on the pathway to its current public popularity through reflection on issues raised by medical practice. The current wave of interest in medical ethics really began just after the last World War, and one of the seminal early works was the book *Medicine and Morals*, published by the Episcopalian priest and theologian Joseph Fletcher, more famous now for his "situation ethics". Fletcher's book had a significant impact on the way both philosophers and theologians discussed medical practice and in the 1960s a debate arose over experimentation using human subjects. Theologians were once again primary contributors. Key contributions were made through the 1960s and '70s from such theologians as Paul Ramsey, James Gustafson, Richard McCormick and Charles Curran. However, by the late '70s the contributions of theologians were clearly on the wane, and as Gustafson noted at that time, even where they continued to contribute there was rarely any explicit appeal to theological or religious claims. This, many would say, is how it should be. However, it might give us some pause for thought when we realize that the dominance of philosophers in the debate was short lived. By the early mid-1990s the dominant voices in medical ethics had become lawyers.

One of the reasons given for this change away from theology is that the voices of philosophers, being based on reason, could appeal to publicly accepted criteria in a way that theologians could not. It is certainly true that theologians became increasingly aware of the need to articulate their thought in a context where their underlying religious assumptions were not widely shared. In order to be heard, theologians ceased to appeal to specifically theological categories, but as they did so their voices became less distinctive. Theologians ceased, qua theologians, to be interesting dialogue partners. Paradoxically, one result of this is that pluralism was excluded from public policy debate out of respect for pluralism. In the interests of "rationality" preference was given to the culturally and historically particular values of the European Enlightenment. Yet as Charles Taylor, Alasdair MacIntyre and others have pointed out, these values too had a clearly religious context and origin. What is more, insofar as they were offered as rational "grounds" for the moral life they were, at best, incomplete.

Perhaps the dominant ethical theory of our age is utilitarianism. Broadly, this theory seeks to give an account of the moral life based solely on empirical observation and reason. The empirical observation is that human behaviour is driven by two masters: the pursuit of pleasure and the avoidance of pain. This is, of course, a hedonistic psychological theory, but it is made to support a moral theory in which we seek not our own pleasure, but rather seek the greatest good for the greatest number. In other words, we are to seek to maximize pleasure and minimize pain in a way that treats the pleasure and pain of each individual equally. We are to act on a principle of beneficence. Now the question that occurs to me at this point is how, on the grounds of reason and empirical observation alone, did we get from hedonism to altruism? What is striking is that neither Jeremy Bentham nor J.S. Mill, the early proponents of this theory, even raises the question.

The most obvious way to make this leap, if we are to ground the theory empirically, would be to claim what is often called "a harmony of interests". In other words we claim that if you seek to maximize the pleasure not just of yourself, but of everyone, your own pleasure will be maximized. The problem with this approach is that it is only really believable within a very narrow and privileged social location. In truth, all too often good people suffer, either because of the malice and wickedness of others, or simply through the indifference of others. My point is that Bentham and Mill did not give evidence, rational or empirical, for the move to beneficence. They simply assumed it. It was a value too deeply embedded in their culture. It was taken for granted, along with the other moral commitments for which utilitarianism was supposed to provide a rational basis.

I need to go on to remind you that Kant defined his moral theories not simply in contrast to the theories of utilitarian moralists, but in flat contradiction. Kant was appalled by the attempt to ground moral commitment in self-interest, prudence or anything else outside the good will. He too sought to provide a theory of the moral life based on reason alone. Yet his theory, like the theories of utilitarianism, has not attracted the support that would suggest that he has succeeded in giving us a purely rational basis for the moral life.

So my point briefly here is that the duality between reason and religious faith is inadequate. It is inadequate because it does not pay sufficient attention to the ways in which religious faith has contributed to the values we all share. It is inadequate because it ascribes a unitary character to the rationalities that shape our culture, which does not stand up to closer scrutiny.

The real challenge for public policy debate arises from the fact that both within groups of religious believers and amongst the wider community of those who are not religious believers, there is an inescapable diversity of ways in which individuals understand the goods at stake in the debate and a variety of conclusions about how to balance their competing demands. We are all shaped by the backgrounds from which we have come and all bring assumptions to our thinking that are not entirely transparent even to ourselves. This leads to diversity both amongst religious believers and within the communities of non-believers. The issue is not secularism; the issue is pluralism.

If this is the reality, then the situation for public policy formation seems bleak enough already and we may indeed find ourselves wondering how the contributions of theologians and religious believers can possibly do anything other than make matters worse.

Perhaps I can put the question differently; perhaps the issue is not people of faith participating in debates concerning public policy, perhaps the question is why religious *institutions* such as churches might be involved. There are good reasons to be suspicious of church involvement. Churches have often functioned as a special interest group that has appeared eager to foist its own religious values on a wider community. Yet this legitimate concern needs to be balanced with recognition of the very real ongoing presence and contribution of churches. In my mind, the marginalization of the church from the corridors of power is healthy; churches have always functioned better as loyal opposition than as government. Yet when we describe churches as special interest groups, it is a description that could be equally applied to political parties or environmental organizations. Yet no other voluntary organization gathers anywhere near the number of people week by week as the churches gather. Any political party that could bring together so many members on a regular basis would consider itself electorally invincible. The Sierra Club of Canada, a significant and influential environmental lobby group has 10,000 members. Even the Anglican Church of Canada has close to one million identifiable givers! It is not surprising that NGOs and even government agencies have begun to look at the infrastructure of religious organizations as a means of reaching grass roots communities. Further, on issues as wide-ranging as climate change, health care reform and international debt, churches and ecumenical advocacy groups have played a pivotal and effective role in mobilizing public opinion through grass roots participation.

At the same time we need to recognize that churches do not speak with one voice. This is certainly true in the area of euthanasia and physician-assisted suicide. Many of you will be aware that recently a retired Anglican priest travelled with his wife from Atlantic Canada to Switzerland where it was legal for his wife to receive assistance to end her own life. In my own Church there would be a diversity of perspectives, and indeed the tone of the report published by the General Synod of the Anglican Church of Canada in 1999 was only cautiously negative in its assessment of the pressure to legalize euthanasia and assisted suicide in Canada. Its focus was less on policy and more on the question of the nature of care. Anglicans are not of one mind. The report acknowledged that fact and assumed that this would be true into the imaginable future. Even churches that have more clearly defined official views have memberships that reflect significant diversity. There is similar diversity in the wider society, and there are other interest groups who have been active in opposing the legalization of euthanasia, in particular groups that represent people with disabilities.

Yet if churches reflect a similar diversity to that found in the surrounding culture, the question needs to be addressed

again: what value can be found from their intervention? I want
to propose three broad areas of participation that might be helpful in a pluralistic context such as ours.

The first contribution I want to propose has to do with
the clarification of assumptions that underlie our debates. In
saying this I am not speaking of the sort of values clarification or
even conceptual clarification that is the work of philosophers.
What I have in mind is, in the context of our interminable
debates, how we acquire the sort of language that will help us
think about the underlying character of our society. I have
already drawn attention to the importance of religious presuppo-
sitions, but in doing this I am not simply saying that there is an
underlying theological basis that in the end we would all have to
share.

I am rather saying that our society has been shaped by
traditions, even mythologies of itself that are important for
understanding how our supposedly rational debates actually get
carried forward. In a Canadian context this is particularly clear
in the area of health care provision. This task is difficult because,
of course, these assumptions are not merely conceptual, they are
tied up with iconic figures and events in Canadian history, and
they are so close to us, so much a part of us, that they are often
difficult to see. Yet there is no view from nowhere, and as we are
shaped by the society, we share both its insights and its
inconsistencies and deceptions. But understanding here is more
like understanding a community's myths—the texts and stories
and individuals that shape it—than it is like understanding an
argument—more like theological than philosophical thought.
Religious thinkers have had to be intentional about their understanding of their own communities, with their ambiguities, their
gift and shadow.

This intentionality has provided the groundwork for the
tools to do that in the context of our wider cultural debates. The
task of the religious contribution here would be to tell the stories
of the underlying and shared values of a society in a way that
gives greater clarity to the values and commitments we share, not
just to affirm those accounts, but also to expose their inconsistencies and deceptions.

The second possible area of contribution relates to the
provision of more adequately rich accounts of the moral life than

those provided by much contemporary theory. In saying this, I want to draw a distinction between the normative role of moral theory and its descriptive role. When Kant defined his theories he was seeking to tell us how we ought to think about the moral life. He was seeking to give us a rational grounding for morals. A different way of thinking about moral theory is to understand its task as primarily descriptive. Its task is not to tell us how we should live the moral life, but to provide an adequate description of the experience of the moral life. If the task is normative, you have to choose between utilitarianism and Kantian deontology—they can't both be true. Yet for most of us we would say that each of them captures some aspect of the moral life and neither is fully adequate. We all agree that we should consider the conse-quences of our actions but "maximizing utility" does not always get at it. It is not always right that "one man should die rather than the whole people perish" Perhaps I can illustrate this differently. The account of freedom, which dominates much of the debate around choices concerning the end of life, is one that has its own history. It comes from the work of Emanuel Kant and his conception of moral agency as rational, disembodied and detached. Immediately, it should be obvious that these qualities are not those that we normally associate with our experience of the medical context. When we present ourselves to a doctor we are more likely to be quite conscious of our embodiment and the reality that something is not well with our bodies. We are also likely to be anxious, and in our anxieties and pain we are not always rational. Kant's theory provides a very neat account of moral agency, but one might question whether it is sufficiently textured to illuminate actual moral decision-making in real moral situations. Again, in the context of the euthanasia debate we are often told to focus on actions, not on the intentions that frame those actions. But is that really possible? Can we really talk about acts without intentions? Isn't an intention what distinguishes an act from a mere reflex?

In our cultural context, and following Kant, freedom is often articulated simply as the right of individuals to choose, unconstrained by any influences outside of themselves. Yet in the context of severe medical illness do we even approximate this? Are we not commonly constrained by the circumstances in which we find ourselves, the very circumstances in which we must decide? In the end it seems to me that ours is a society that over-plays the role of the will in the formation of human persons. It tends to obscure both the influences that shape how we exercise our wills and also the significantly different access to goods, to opportunities, and therefore to choices, that different individuals actually have. In the context of considerations of euthanasia there is considerable evidence from Canadian studies that one of the key factors in predicting a stated desire to have the option of assisted suicide is the sense of being a burden on others (40%). This is significant, and it is a factor that inevitably has social correlates. It will be a bigger factor for some than for others. My point here is not to argue for or against legalization of euthan-asia, only to say that the discussion needs to be based on under-standings of human will and human motives that are richer and more insightful than those often appealed to on either side of the debate. Religious categories, while not shared by all, may be helpful if they enable us to provide particularly rich and nuanced accounts of widely held consensus. The task of the church in this context is not to foist its views on others, but to identify the sources of core shared values and then to deploy theological categories to provide an account of those values that is richer and more compelling than alternative accounts.

The frustration for public policy formation is that this will not always yield simple and clear results. This should not surprise us because the reality of the moral life is that it is not clean. It is not simple, and solutions are, at best, about balancing complex claims that cannot all be realized. Given this, it is not surprising that so much ethical discourse is, in fact, cast in the form of debate. Indeed, Alasdair MacIntyre has noted that this debate appears to be interminable, not simply in the sense that it goes on and on without end, but more specifically in the sense that it has no terminus, no commonly agreed ground upon which it could be concluded. This is why moral issues are so frustrating from a public policy perspective. But despite our frustrations we need to pay attention not simply to moral outcomes, but also to the manner in which decisions are reached.

At this point I would like to suggest a distinction between the debates that characterize most of our public policy discus-sions, and dialogue. Put simply, debate by its very nature has winners and losers. The purpose of debate is to clarify truth and separate it from positions that are erroneous or incomplete. Debate privileges assertion whereas, by contrast, dialogue privileges relationship. Dialogue begins in the recognition of relationship and shared values. It is not, in the first place, about winners and losers, but about relationship and mutual responsibility. To understand debate it is enough to explain the basic premises at stake for each side. To understand a dialogue it is important to understand the community that shapes and is shaped by that dialogue.

The third and final contribution that I would suggest religious thinkers and religious communities might offer would be some significant insights into the practices that make possible and sustain moral community. Too often, philosophical ethicists seem to imply that moral decision-making is a basically intellectual practice, and therefore a practice in which they have particular expertise. But there is little evidence that a good ethical argument ever made anyone more moral. If that were the case, one would expect ethicists to be more moral than the rest of us and, sadly, there is empirical evidence to the contrary. So the question is, how do we, in fact, learn to negotiate the complexities and challenges of the moral life? How might we effectively undertake moral pedagogy?

This is a huge challenge for education at present. Not infrequently some public leader complains that children are not being taught right from wrong and some other public figure replies that they are being given a moral education as they are taught to articulate how they make their decisions, which is all that is possible in the context of pluralism. But this is nonsense. It ignores the very real and, I would argue, robust cross-cultural consensus on many matters. It is hard to imagine a society that views murder or theft as goods. The difficulty is that consensus is not something we notice as easily as disagreement because we are not provoked to discuss it. What we urgently need at this time are patterns of moral discourse that do not elide these areas of agreement that are so important if we are to address the more contested issues. Such practices would need to be more dialogical and less debate-oriented. The problem with debate is that it privileges assertion and argument over relationship. Dialogue begins in a recognition and affirmation of relationship and what it is we share together.

111

In addition to moral pedagogy and some rethinking about how we structure our moral discourses in ways that support rather than undermine moral community, I think we need to pay attention to what happens when the good life fails. What do we do when the moral community is fractured? It is true that somebody has acted in a way that is destructive, but what then? We can punish if the act is illegal, but the real challenge is to recognize the impact on our common life and work out ways to restore moral community after it has been broken. To say that Robert Latimer acted inappropriately, as I believe in the end we must, is only to say the first and, in some ways the least interesting thing. The questions that must follow need to be about what next. And those questions need to take seriously the way in which the options and choices available to Mr. Latimer and his family were options that were limited by decisions made by the rest of us. These questions also make clear the complete inadequacy of systems of mandatory sentencing that in this case prevented the judiciary from taking account of significant elements of the case and from passing judgment in ways that showed sensitivity to them.

In the face of tragedies such as this, religious thought does not, it seems to me, bring a unique set of insights and moral claims to public discourse (we have the same diversities as the rest of Canadian society). It certainly should not seek to impose a religious solution on a wider Canadian society (we can't even impose solutions on ourselves most of the time as is obvious in current Anglican debates about homosexuality). What it can do is live out of its capacity to be intentional about the communal context of moral discourse. For theologians moral discourse cannot in the end simply be a matter of who is right and who is wrong and how we know that. For those whose intellectual context is a community of faith, these questions are important, but they are framed by other, wider questions. What makes for sustainable moral community? How do we engage in moral pedagogy? That is, how do we assist people in their growth in the moral life? And finally, what do we do when the moral life goes wrong, when moral community is fractured?

This call to restore community has nothing to do with simplistic notions of forgiving and forgetting. It does have to do with remembering in ways that make future community possible.

I am struck by what I take to be one of the most striking examples of this in the public arena in modern times, namely the Truth and Reconciliation Commission in South Africa. It was built on the theological insight that truth-telling is what sets us free. That telling the truth of the appalling things we sometimes do to each other, for the worst of motives and for the best, is the first step in moving past those events into new and very differently structured community. It came out of a sense that something had to be done to prevent South Africa from collapsing into civil war. It was an act both religious and public, an act where the task for religious leadership was not to impose their perspective, but to allow people to tell their own stories in ways that held open the door for reconciliation and renewal. Theologians would call this a redemptive moment. Non-theologians may want another word for it. Yet it is and needs to be the experience of human individuals and human societies when they are brought to the end of their resources and beyond.

Notes on the Contributors

Compiled by David Buley, editor

TERRY WAITE (CBE) is a British-born humanitarian and author who, in the 1980s, was Archbishop of Canterbury Robert Runcie's Assistant for Anglican Communion Affairs. As an envoy for the Church of England, he travelled to Lebanon in an attempt to secure the release of four hostages held captive there. He was himself held as a hostage between 1987 and 1991. Mr. Waite has been awarded numerous honorary doctorates and is in high demand as a speaker. He is President of the charity Y Care International (the YMCA's international development and relief agency) and Patron of AbleChildAfrica. He is a contributor to *Guantánamo: What the World Should Know* (Arris, 2004) and is the author of *Taken on Trust* (Coronet, 1994) and *Footfalls in Memory: Reflections from Solitude* (Coronet, 1996) as well as the humourous set of tales, *Travels with a Primate* (Harper-Collins, 2001).

JOCELYN DOWNIE (BA, MA, MLitt, LLB, LLM, SJD, FRSC) is the Canada Research Chair in Health Law and Policy in the Faculties of Law and Medicine at Dalhousie University in Halifax, Nova Scotia. Long at the forefront of the intersection of law, ethics and health care, Ms. Downie's work has been focused on contributing to the academic literature and affecting change in health law and policy at the federal and provincial levels in Canada. Her book *Dying Justice: A Case of Decriminalizing Euthanasia and Assisted Suicide in Canada* (University of Toronto Press, 2004) has become an important piece of the debate surrounding ends-of-life concerns, and she is a co-editor of *Canadian Health Law and Policy*, 4th edition (Lexis-Nexis, 2010).

KAREN LEBACQZ (BA, MA, PhD) possesses a life-long commitment to issues of social justice that have surfaced in the areas of professional ethics, bioethics and ethical theory. Her publications include *Six Theories of Justice* (Augsburg Fortress, 2005) and *Justice in an Unjust World* (Augsburg Fortress, 1990) and she is a co-author of *Ethics and Spiritual Care* (Abingdon, 2000). Her numerous essays in bioethics, feminist ethics and sexual ethics have been published in scientific journals, church magazines and international contexts and she has contributed articulately to the important and lively debate around these themes. Dr. Lebacqz is an ordained minister in the United Church of Christ and is Professor Emerita of Theological Ethics at the Pacific School of Religion and the Graduate Theological Union in Berkeley, California.

HARVEY M. CHOCHINOV (OM, MD, PhD, FRCPC, FRSC) holds the only Canada Research Chair in Palliative Care and is a recipient of the Queen's Golden Jubilee Medal and the Order of Manitoba for his work in palliative care. He is Head of Patient and Family Support Services at CancerCare Manitoba, Distinguished Professor of Psychiatry at the University of Manitoba, and is an important contributor to ideas about ethics and quality of medical care at the ends of life. He is the co-editor of two editions of the *Handbook of Psychiatry in Palliative Medicine* (Oxford University Press, 2000 and 2009) and of the journal *Palliative and Supportive Care*. Dr. Chochinov is Chair of the Canadian Virtual Hospice, a bilingual website dedicated to providing assistance to families and health professionals dealing with end-of-life concerns (http://www.virtualhospice.ca).

GENEVIEVE THOMPSON (RN, PhD, CHPCN(C)) is a post-doctoral fellow with the Manitoba Palliative Care Research Unit. She completed her Bachelor of Nursing degree in 1997 and her PhD in Community Health Sciences in 2007, both at the University of Manitoba. Her research is focused on understanding the palliative care needs of persons with dementia and their family caregivers. It examines the issues and challenges in delivering quality palliative/end-of-life care to older adults living in long-term care facilities. Dr. Thompson's interest is in developing predictive models of satisfaction with end-of-life care, communication tools to facilitate end-of-life discussions, the assessment of quality care at life's end and understanding the needs of family caregivers.

ALLAN E. BLAKENEY (PC, OC, SOM, QC, FRSC) was the Premier of Saskatchewan from 1971 to 1982, and leader of the Saskatchewan New Democratic Party. Originally from Nova Scotia, Mr. Blakeney was a Rhodes Scholar. Upon returning to Canada, he entered the Saskatchewan Civil Service, then was elected a member of the Saskatchewan Government led by Tommy Douglas. He was appointed Minister of Health, thus playing a crucial role in the introduction of Medicare. Mr. Blakeney was an Officer of the Order of Canada and a recipient of the Saskatchewan Order of Merit. A Fellow of the Royal Society of Canada, he was past president of the Canadian Civil Liberties Association.

ERIC BERESFORD (BSc, BA, MA, Certificate in Theology, DD *honoris causa*) is the President of the Atlantic School of Theology in Halifax, as well as a scholar and prolific writer. He is widely published in professional journals and sought after as a consultant and speaker at workshops and conferences in the fields of ethics, environmental justice, conflict and change, and human sexuality. Canon Beresford is an ordained Anglican priest who has served parishes in England and Canada and continues to serve on national committees of the Anglican Church of Canada.

INNIS CHRISTIE (LLB, Dip CLS, LLM, QC) was a highly respected Nova Scotia mediator-arbitrator, teacher and mentor who enjoyed a distinguished career as a professor and dean of the Dalhousie Law School, specializing in employment law. In addition to his academic work he served as Chair of the Labour Relations Board in Nova Scotia. As Deputy Minister of Labour for the Nova Scotia Government, his work was seminal in establishing the NS Occupational Health and Safety Act. Innis Christie also served as Chair of the NS Workers' Compensation Board and was instrumental in creating the NS Trade Union Act and the Labour Standards Code. Contributing to academic work in labour law, he authored *The Liability of Strikers in the Law of Tort* (Queen's University Press, 1967) and his book *Employment Law in Canada* (Butterworths, 1980) became a standard text on the subject. His numerous rulings in the realm of labour arbitration won him a place of extraordinary respect, and in 2008 he was honoured as a recipient of the University of Toronto's Bora Laskin Award for outstanding contributions to labour law in Canada, as well as the Nova Scotia Barristers' Society Distinguished Service Award.

DAVID STUEWE (BA, MA, PhD) is the chair of the Segelberg Trust Board of Directors as well as a professor of public administration and business administration in the Faculty of Management at Dalhousie University. His research interests include governance of independent public agencies and he is active in numerous community organizations including the Big Cove YMCA Camp Advisory Committee.

DAVID BULEY (Editor) (BA, BEd, MMus, MPhil, PhD) is an assistant professor of music education and education law in the Concurrent Education Program at Laurentian University in Sudbury, Ontario. He also teaches Christian worship and hymnology through the Thorneloe College School of Theology at Thorneloe University in Sudbury.

THE SEGELBERG TRUST was originally established in 1984 by the Reverend Doctor Eric Segelberg to assist academic studies and research, particularly relating to studies in theology and church matters. In 1995, the Segelberg Trust refocused its objectives to promote theological conferences, religious education and, in particular, reaching out to youth who might not otherwise be exposed to the contribution of spirituality and formal religion. Recently, the Segelberg Trust has expanded its objectives to promote ongoing debate among the areas of theology, public policy and the environment. For current information please see: http://www.segelbergtrust.ca